W9-CPM-251

# 100 GREATEST WOMEN IN SPORTS

# About the Author

A graduate of the University of Michigan and an avid sportswoman, Phyllis Hollander is senior editor of Associated Features Inc., packagers of sports books. Her writing credits include *American Women in Sports* and chapters in *They Dared to Lead* and *Strange But True Football Stories*, which she coedited with her sportswriter husband, Zander. She also coedited *The Complete Book of Cheerleading* (Doubleday) with L. R. Herkimer.

The Hollanders, who have a son and daughter, work in New York City and live in the Dutchess County community of Millerton, New York.

# 100 GREATEST WOMEN IN SPORTS

## BY PHYLLIS HOLLANDER
An Associated Features Book

**Illustrated With Photographs**

Publishers · GROSSET & DUNLAP · New York
A FILMWAYS COMPANY

796
Hol

For Alice and Tobye, who each played the game in her own special way . . . and emerged a champion.

1978 PRINTING

# CONTENTS

# Introduction

What better time to review women's accomplishments in the field of sports than during the first International Women's Year. It is a time to look back, tally up, and forge ahead. Much is still to be done if women around the world are to achieve the full scope of their potential as human beings and contributing citizens.

While we searched the past, it became apparent to us that although it has taken a long time, women athletes have made great strides — particularly in the last ten years, when more women and girls have been free to play their own game.

This book includes modern-day crusaders, like Billie Jean King, tennis-libber; Kathy Kusner, the first woman in this country to obtain a jockey's license; and Nina Kuscsik, the first women's division winner of the previously all-male Boston Marathon — and pioneers of the past.

Their stories, often filled with now-broken records, will remain a part of the history of the growing strength of women all over the world. All-around athlete Eleonora Sears, who spurned high society to do her own thing; American tennis queen Helen Wills, who shocked England and its queen when she bared her legs at Wimbledon; and gray-haired Floretta McCutcheon, who brought bowling out of the dark "alleys" onto the swinging lanes are people who will never be forgotten.

All these athletes, of the past or of the present, could be called "liberated." They have followed their own star in spite of the restrictions of society, inadequate coaching, lack of finances, or the myth of the weaker sex. Some were school girls who managed to fulfill their educational goals while achieving champion status (Helen Wills was a Phi Beta Kappa, and Tenley Albright became a surgeon). Others were housewives, mothers, and grandmothers who stretched their capacities to bear and raise children while winning titles (golfer Glenna Collett, runner Fanny Blankers-Koen, or tennis star Margaret Court). And some were athletes of single-minded purpose, who just wanted to be the best in their field.

Many of today's athletes are seeking equality with men on a professional level. Why, they ask, shouldn't a woman earn a living in sports if she chooses? Pros like golfer Sandra Palmer, tennis player Chrissie Evert, and figure skater Janet Lynn are already showing it can be done.

Of the more than one hundred women highlighted here about twenty or so rose to glory before 1950. In addition to Americans, there are athletes from a dozen other countries. You will find heroines in twenty different sports — from baseball, basketball, and bicycling to swimming, track, and volleyball. And, believe it or not, their ages range from the early teens to more than a hundred years old!

The tales told are of stars of every kind . . . short and tall, rich and poor, old and young, married and single. It is a credit to the strength and perseverance of women that this book is able to include more than *One Hundred Greatest Women in Sports.*

# BASKETBALL

## Through the Hoop

- **DONNA CHAIT**
- **MARIANNE CRAWFORD**
- **KAREN LOGAN**
- **DENISE LONG**
- **DEBBY MASON**
- **MARY SCHARFF**

Basketball was invented in this country in 1891, and a year later the women of America came out to play. Today swishing the ball through the hoop continues to be one of the most popular activities for women since the peach basket was the goal.

In addition to competitions in schools and colleges, organized games have been sponsored by just about every type of organization — social, religious, industrial. One of America's greatest athletes started her sporting career as a basketball player for the Golden Cyclones, a team sponsored by the Employers Casualty Company of Dallas, Texas. Mildred "Babe" Didrikson led her team to the championship in 1931, when she scored 106 points in five tournament games. She was selected for the All-American team from 1930 through 1932 before going on to conquer new worlds in track and field, and golf.

It was not until 1976 that women's basketball was included in the schedule for the Olympics but it has been a popular sport at the Pan-American Games since 1955, with United States teams generally dominating.

Women's basketball came into its own when, in February, 1975, the leading college teams of the AIAW (Association for Intercollegiate Athletics for Women) met in New York City's Madison Square Garden for the first time. Before a vociferous crowd of 12,000 fans, the Mighty Macs from Immaculata College in Philadelphia met the Queens College (New York) Knightees. It was a night full of the usual Garden hoopla — banners, pompons, cheerleaders, and superior ball-handling. It was an exciting game, led by star athletes Donna Chait and Debby "the Pearl" Mason (Queens), and Mary Scharff and Marianne Crawford (Immaculata).

The Mighty Macs emerged victorious, 65–61. Coach Cathy Rush, who had led Immaculata to the national championships four years in a row, became the spokeswoman for the strategies and techniques of the women's game. "We have played the game well and in so doing have proved that people will pay to see women play basketball," she commented.

People have been paying to see women play an exhibition brand of basketball since 1936, in fact, when a team called the All-American World's Champion Girls

*Karen Logan, champion basketball player, leaps the hurdles in the first Women's Superstar competition at Rotonda, Florida, in January, 1975.*          UPI

*An Iowa high school star, Denise Long was drafted by the San Francisco Warriors in 1969, but National Basketball Association Commissioner Walter Kennedy would not allow it.*          UPI

Basketball Club started touring the country, spoofing the sport. One year (1947), it was reported that the group had played in forty-six states after having traveled some 30,000 miles. In 1971, under the new name of the Red Heads, they won 169 games, playing according to men's rules against all-male teams. Accomplished athletes, the girls dyed their hair red and, with a touch of whimsy, skillfully handled the ball to shoot it up much like those colorful wizards of the court, the Harlem Globe Trotters.

Perhaps the finest athlete ever to play for the Red Heads was California-born Karen Logan. She had excelled in a wide range of sports and because of her natural ability was compared to the great Babe Didrikson. Karen was number one singles player on the Pepperdine College tennis team, and might have made the Olympics

in 1968 as a 400-meter runner if a pulled tendon hadn't caused her to withdraw.

She proved her all-around ability in 1975, when she appeared in the finals of the first women's Superstar competition at Rotonda, Florida. In ten events, including swimming, tennis, bowling, bicycling, running, throwing, and rowing (she was excluded from the basketball), Karen piled up a total of 38 points and $13,800 for her runner-up placing.

Twenty-five-year-old Ms. Logan returned to the basketball court, playing for a professional team based near Indianapolis, Indiana. The team, known as the Pink Panthers, billed the now-blonde Karen as the number one woman basketball player in America. Once again playing mostly against men, Karen toured the country, averaging 23 points a game.

Women's basketball has traveled many

miles, trying to prove its identity. There is still a long way to go. There are few other professional opportunities for top women hoopsters. When Frank Mieuli tried to draft high school star Denise Long for his San Francisco Warriors, the National Basketball Association would not allow it. Denise, a 5 foot 11 inch jump shooter from Union, Iowa, once scored 111 points in a girls' high school game and had tallied a career total of 6,250 points. The NBA must have been looking for an 8 foot center.

*Immaculata's high scorer, Mary Scharff, is on the ball in the first girls' basketball game ever played at Madison Square Garden, New York, on February 22, 1975.*  WIDE WORLD

# BICYCLING

## The Spokeswomen

- **SUE NOVARA**
- **JEAN ROBINSON**
- **SHEILA YOUNG**

Bicycling is probably America's most popular participant sport, the cyclists including tykes on their first "trikes" to senior citizens pedaling their own version of the same tricycle. In between are the millions of men and women on two-wheelers who enjoy the sport for mental and physical relaxation, for exercise and weight control, or for just getting where they want to go.

As for outstanding women cyclists, however, there haven't been many, perhaps because bicycle riding had so long been considered a leisure-time diversion and not a competitive activity.

But in 1973 a young woman from Detroit accomplished a most extraordinary feat. Twenty-three-year-old Sheila Young became the first athlete ever to win world championships in track cycling and speed skating as well.

Sheila, who was coached by her father, began cycling in order to train for a career in speed skating. Although many athletes use the bicycle as an off-season conditioner, few have the stamina and determination to enter the arena of competitive cycling.

On February 24 and 25 in Stromsund,

Sweden, Sheila won the world 500-meter speed skating event. Six months later, in San Sebastian, Spain, she became the first American woman since 1912 to win a world cycling track championship. Before the year was out, Sheila set the world record for the 500-meter speed skating sprint (47.8) and earned her second crown in the U.S. Amateur Bicycle League's national track championships.

Sheila's greatest triumph, however, occurred in speed skating in the 1976 Winter Olympics in Innsbruck, Austria. The twenty-five-year-old athlete became the first from the United States to bring home three medals from the Winter Games — gold in the 500 meters, silver in the 1500, and bronze in the 1000.

Interestingly enough, another champion cyclist came into competition by way of another sport. Seattle's Jean Robinson was a cross-country runner in the early 1970s. Her research job as a primatologist at the University of Washington gave her much insight into training and diet. Her interest in competitive cycling led her to pedal 35 to 50 miles a day, five days a week!

At the 1974 Women's National Road

*In 1973, Sheila Young, champion track cyclist and speed skater, became the first athlete to win world crowns in both sports.* WIDE WORLD

*Nineteen-year-old Sue Novara won a world championship in sprint cycling in Belgium in 1975.* WIDE WORLD

Championships in Pontiac, Michigan, the course was crowded with contestants, forty-five at the starting line. An accident caused a pile-up just a few pedals from the start, with everyone jamming for up-front positions, and several women went down amid spinning wheels and cries of pain. Later on, in the last leg of the 34.5 mile event another spill occurred. In the confusion, a tiny red-skirted rider pulled ahead of the pack and pedaled to victory. Unknown twenty-seven-year-old, 5 foot tall Jean Robinson was the new dark-horse champion.

A week later in Northbook, Illinois, another form of cycling competition was held. The National Track Racing Championships, short-distance events tested speed, judgment, and experience rather than chance and endurance. The two leaders of the competition were past champions of the Match Sprint event — Sheila Young and Sue Novara. In 1971 Shiela won the title. In 1972 Sue took it. In 1973 Sheila won it back. Now the crowd waited eagerly for the results of the 1974 all-out struggle.

Between cries of "Go, Sue" and "Ride 'em, Sheila," the fans were transfixed on the whirling cyclists. It was a close ride, with Sue Novara crossing the finish line a half-wheel ahead.

Nineteen-year-old Sue also went on to capture the first gold medal in sprint cycling in the 1975 world championships in Belgium. America once again could claim a champion spokeswoman in its most popular leisure sport.

# BOWLING

## The Pied Piper of Bowling

## • FLORETTA McCUTCHEON

Although bowling is a sport that dates back to the Egyptians in 5200 B.C., the bowling "alley" in America was once considered a disreputable place for ladies. Even fifty years ago, women bowled at the risk of losing their reputations, most often in dark, secluded basements behind heavy concealing drapes. It was as difficult to get women out to the alleys as it was to find husbands who would allow their wives to bowl.

One of the earliest and most honored women bowlers, one who dared to venture out onto the "dark alleys," was Floretta McCutcheon. She was born in 1888 in Ottumwa, Iowa. Floretta didn't pick up a bowling ball until thirty-five years later, when she was a housewife in Pueblo, Colorado.

Floretta had turned prematurely gray and disliked her plump, matronly appearance. Perhaps, she thought, if she lost some weight she could regain her youthful looks. A friend suggested bowling as a good form of exercise.

The first time she lifted the 16-pound ball, Floretta was ready to quit. It took a lot of persistence to finish the game with an unimpressive score of 69. For the next few years Floretta continued to play. Although she never lost her motherly appearance, her game took on the quality of youth.

In 1926, Jimmy Smith, the world champion bowler and national match champion for eight years, came to Pueblo for an exhibition game. Floretta, by this time the best bowler of her community, watched Jimmy's technique carefully.

"I'd been a self-taught bowler," she said, "because there were no instructors in those days. I tried to alter my style to fit his."

Jimmy returned to Pueblo a year later. This time the owner of the bowling alley took him aside. "Want to meet one of our local players?" he asked.

"Glad to, where is he?" Jimmy parried.

"She," replied the proprietor, pointing to Floretta.

The confrontation became bowling history. Jimmy rolled three strong games for a total of 687 points. Floretta's three games totaled 704. It was the highest series ever bowled against champion Jimmy Smith and he admitted with some embarrassment that the thirty-nine-year-old housewife was one of the greatest bowlers he had ever met.

Jimmy's manager Carl Cain, recognizing the drawing value of a woman bowler, offered to organize an exhibition and teaching tour for Floretta. Anxious to raise money to send her daughter Barbara through the University of Colorado, Floretta accepted.

Floretta's tours lasted over a decade — until 1939 — during which time she piled up an impressive list of records. Many of them do not appear in official record books because they were scored in either instructional exhibitions or in unsanctioned match play. All of them, however, have been accepted as a part of bowling history.

In one series of exhibitions, Floretta averaged 248 for twelve games. She bowled a three-game record high of 832 in 1931. She recorded ten perfect 300 games and nine at 299. Her ten-year average in over

eight thousand games was 201, with a 206 average during the 1938–39 season.

Floretta, however, was not just a great bowler; she was also respected as an organizer and instructor. Wherever she went she set up bowling leagues and bowling schools. Mrs. Mac, as she was called, was a warm, sincere woman — silver-haired and stocky — who looked more like a woman who had just stepped out of the kitchen than out of a bowling lane. Women had faith in her. If she could do it, why not they? Floretta, the Pied Piper of women's bowling, was credited with having taught over 250,000 women and children from the ages of eight to eighty.

When Floretta died in 1966 at the age of seventy-eight, Mrs. Juanita Rich of Los Angeles, an official of the Women's Bowling Association, said: "I don't think anybody will ever set records like Mrs. McCutcheon did. And she bowled under such adverse conditions . . . when 'alleys' really were 'alleys.'"

*This was the way it was in the days of Floretta McCutcheon.*                    UPI

# Down the Lane With Grandma

## • MARION LADEWIG

Marion Ladewig spelled her first name with an "O" like a boy because her mother had wanted a boy. But Marion was far from being boyish in manner or appearance. For as long as she was bowling, when she appeared on the lanes she was slim, chic, and carefully coiffured. It was not unusual to hear whistles along with the applause as the 5 foot 4 inch, 124-pound blonde added championship to championship.

The glamorous Mrs. Ladewig was the first woman to win the BPAA (Bowling Proprietors Association of America) Women's All-Star title in 1949. She won it again in 1950, and when she returned to the eight-day tournament the following year, Marion put on one of the most outstanding performances in the sport's history. For two days she struggled in second place before zooming ahead to victory. She rolled consecutive games of 255 and 279, a two-game All-Star record that still stands. Her astonishing average at the end of the eight days was 247.5 — topping everyone in the tournament, including 160 men.

In the years that followed, Marion won the All-Star event an unprecedented total of eight times. She won the World Invitational crown five times, the National Doubles twice, and the Women's International Bowling Congress All-Events title twice. The Bowling Writers Association of America chose her Woman Bowler of the Year nine times.

In the 1963 Associated Press Woman Athlete of the Year poll, she was ranked third after golfer Mickey Wright and tennis champion Maria Bueno. Although stars of swimming, tennis, golf, and track had all produced "athletes of the year," this marked the first time a bowler even came close to this designation. Marion Ladewig had made bowling a recognized sport.

In November, 1965, Marion stepped up to the line in a Chicago bowling establishment. She took careful aim and rolled her last ball in the World Invitational Tournament. Cheers and clapping echoed through the hall for those who were fortunate enough to be there to witness the fifth and final tournament victory of the amazing Mrs. Ladewig. Several weeks later, Marion, by then the trim and attractive grandmother of five, announced her

*Youthful-looking Marion Ladewig, "Woman Bowler of the Year" nine times, had been a grand-mother for a decade before retiring from competition in 1965.*

retirement from tournament competition.

She was half-a-century old. She had dominated the bowling scene for nearly twenty years, winning virtually every major bowling title during that time. Her man-sized average over those years was 190.

At the height of her career, Mrs. Ladewig earned over $25,000 a year from bowling. She commanded $150 a day for exhibitions, wrote a syndicated "tips" column, acted as a consultant in sportswear design, served on the advisory staff of the Brunswick Corporation and won grand prizes in tournaments.

It was a far cry from the days when she earned $2.50 a day for sweeping up and emptying ashtrays at Morrissey's Fana-torium Lanes in Grand Rapids, Mich-igan. Grandma Marion exemplified the new era in bowling, a sport for young and old, bringing not only health and recre-ation to millions, but for a special few, prosperity as well.

# The Striking Athletes

- CAROL ANDERTON
- JUDY COOK
- PATTY COSTELLO
- DOROTHY FOTHERGILL
- PAULA SPERBER

When the first women's bowling organization was founded in 1916 in St. Louis, Missouri, it had only 40 charter members. The new group, the Women's International Bowling Congress (WIBC), was started to provide and enforce rules of play and to sponsor an annual tournament. At the WIBC's fiftieth anniversary celebration in 1966, there were 2.9 million on its rolls and a decade later the figure had grown to 3.4 million! There could be no doubt that bowling had become women's most popular sport.

During the last decade several notable champions rolled down the lane. Dorothy Fothergill from North Attleboro, Massachusetts, was Woman Bowler of the Year in 1968 and 1969. The following year Dorothy was the Individual and the All-Events champion for the WIBC. By 1973 she had accumulated $39,214 in tournament earnings, which made her the all-time money winner for the Professional Women's Bowling Association (PWBA).

Dotty's roommate on the pro circuit was twenty-six-year-old Patty Costello. This super bowler from New Carrollton, Maryland, won the U.S. Open in 1972 as well as

four other of the eleven major tournaments sponsored by the PWBA. As a youngster, Patty spent all of her spare time at the bowling center near her home. When she was sixteen she was bowling an average of 132. At the top of her form, ten years later, she was rolling 205, which was not too far from the 212 average score of top male bowlers.

Yet, scoring was about the only area in which professional women bowlers approached equality with men. The women complained bitterly over the lack of big-league opportunities in the sport. While the men had at least one major tournament a week to compete in, the women still had only eleven a year. And Judy Cook, who was Top Money Winner in 1972 with $11,200, was compared to men's champion Don McCune, who took home $69,000 in prize monies.

Whatever the differences, the WIBC reported that over 125,000 weekly bowling leagues were in operation around the country. Such local play was what made champions. Judy Cook, a mother of two from Grandview, Missouri, had been a league bowler for many years. In 1973, she

*Paula Sperber bowled a spectacular 290 in the 1966 Algiers Junior Classic when she was only fifteen years old.*                    UPI

*In 1973 Judy Cook made the Professional Women's Bowling Association top average with 207.215*                    UPI

finally ended a string of thirteen runner-up finishes when she won the Pearl Cup in April in Japan. She followed that up with victories in the Ebonite Classic (August) and the Cavalcade of Stars (November). This made her only the fourth woman in bowling history to win consecutive tournaments. When she was selected Bowler of the Year that year, she had earned the PWBA top average with a 207.215.

Perhaps the most striking bowler of this period was a beautiful left-handed blonde from Miami. Paula Sperber had first made Florida headlines in 1966, when as a fifteen-year-old, she bowled an extraordinary 290 game in the Algiers Junior Classic. As the years progressed, Paula's perfect form and figure attracted much attention in tournaments around the country. However, the 5 foot 6 inch, modellike athlete was not just good to look at. In 1971, after only one year on the pro tour, she was selected Bowler of the Year, and by 1974, she had added two U.S. Opens to her credit.

In October, 1975, at the famed Caesars Palace in Las Vegas, Nevada, a woman bowling star finally struck it rich — and not by playing the slot machines. Carol Anderton, a blonde, blue-eyed Texan won the Brunswick Showdown. For her victory in this "Super Bowl" of bowling, Ms. Anderton received $50,000, the biggest prize in the history of the sport!

*Twenty-five-year-old Patty Costello won bowling's U.S. Open in 1972, as well as four other major tournaments.*                    UPI

# FIELD HOCKEY

## An Apple
## for the Coach

### •CONSTANCE APPLEBEE

Constance Applebee, affectionately known as "the Apple" because of her tart, crunchy personality, coached field hockey until she was ninety-five years old and was still spry and feisty at the ripe old age of one hundred and one!

While field hockey is a sport that has never honored its leaders with trophies, medals, or championships, for over sixty-five years there was never any doubt about who was the queen of the fields.

During her reign in America, which began in 1901, when she brought the favorite sport of her native England to this country, the Apple spread the seeds of hockey to more than a million athletes. She taught in over thirty-four nations around the world. In America she coached thousands in junior and senior high schools and colleges as well as about 50,000 in organized clubs and associations.

The energetic Ms. Applebee was also responsible for editing and publishing America's first women's sports magazine while she was coaching at Bryn Mawr College in Pennsylvania. *The Sportswoman*, as the magazine was called, contained, in addition to news in the world of field hoc-

key, articles of interest in such sports as lacrosse, skating, swimming, fencing, and archery.

Ms. Applebee's devotion was to hockey, however, and as the very model of a field-hockey player, she believed her sport could answer most of the problems confronting budding young women. "It develops strong nerves, will power, determination, discipline, and endurance," Coach Applebee told her youthful charges. "It gives a girl physical and mental strength."

And indeed it does, for field hockey is no game for sissies. As in soccer, there are no substitutions or time-outs. It is a hard-hitting, lunging, swerving, running, and tackling game. The women swing their sticks through two 30-minute periods, with only one short rest between.

Although the game was once considered an upper-class pastime, played mainly in the nation's private schools, it has grown in popularity and scope, due largely to the U.S. Field Hockey Association. In 1922, Ms. Applebee presided over a meeting of about one hundred women in Philadelphia to form the USFHA. From the beginning, the organized tournaments of the Association (national and international) refused to recognize its winners as champions. "It might destroy the friendly atmosphere among players and nations."

Field hockey is a sport whose players span the generations. In a 1967 tournament in Glassboro, New Jersey, tournament players ranged in age from nineteen to fifty. The New Atlantic team had four players over forty-five, who were jokingly referred to as the Medicare Squad.

When "the Apple" was one hundred and one years old in 1975, she was living without help in a small cottage in Hants, England. Although her eyesight was failing, she was still sound in body and spirit. She was living proof that her beloved sport did indeed lead to "a splendid, healthful life of vigor and endurance."

*Constance Applebee, field hockey's most illustrious coach and proponent, was still alert and physically fit at one hundred and one.* WIDE WORLD

# FIGURE SKATING
## Mrs. Figure Skater, U.S.A.

### • THERESA WELD BLANCHARD

If twelve-year-old Theresa Weld of Brookline, Massachusetts, hadn't been able to harness and drive her pony and cart the 3 miles to the Skating Club of Boston, she might never have become America's first figure skating champion.

The club, with its exceptional outdoor ice surface, was founded in 1911. Its charter members, including Theresa's father, A. Winsor Weld, were devotees of a new style of figure skating, the International mode — which featured a freer, more fluid way of getting across the ice. Theresa much preferred the new freedom to America's stiff style, so when she finally had permission to harness her pony, she trotted over to the club as often as possible.

When Theresa entered competition in 1914, she became America's first ladies' champion at New Haven, Connecticut. She captured the singles title again from 1920 through 1924 — a total of six times. At those same initial championships, she skated with Nathaniel W. Niles to win the waltz event and come in second to Canadians Jeanne Chevalier and Norman Scott in the pairs. Theresa and Mr. Niles won

nine gold medals in the U.S. pairs competitions, starting in 1924, and the North American title in 1925.

She was the only American skater in those days to do any jumps beyond a toe hop of some sort. Often her daring loops and jumps were actually marked down by some judges for being "unladylike." When Theresa competed in the Olympics in 1920 at Antwerp, Belgium, she won a bronze medal. She got the most overwhelming ovation of her career at that time from the hundreds of United States soldiers who were sitting in the arena stands. Following World War I the American army was still in occupation on the Rhine, and the soldiers presented their home-grown skater with kisses and flowers as well as cheers. From then on, Theresa rarely missed an Olympics in some capacity, either as a competitor or an official. After her marriage to Charles Blanchard in 1920 she was known as Mrs. Figure Skater, U.S.A.

When the U.S. Figure Skating Association was formed in 1921, Theresa's father was elected its first president. The new organization needed an official publication, and the editorial task fell to Mrs.

Blanchard and Mr. Niles. The magazine *Skating*, published for the first time in December, 1923, was still the bible of the sport over fifty years later, and still in the dedicated hands of the untiring "Tee" Blanchard.

In a glowing tribute, to Mrs. Blanchard on her thirtieth anniversary with *Skating* magazine, Dr. James Koch, president of the International Skating Union wrote: "If anyone in our skating family has deserved such honor then it is you . . . for I do not know anybody who has worked with such efficiency, prudence and fine taste for the benefit of skating and has rendered such outstanding service to our sport. . . . I always have been and still am full of admiration for your work."

*Theresa Weld Blanchard become America's first national champion in figure skating in 1914.*

# Skating Into the Movies

## • SONJA HENIE

A blizzard was raging in Chamonix, France, and the howling wind and heavily falling snow forced all the skating competitors at the 1924 Winter Olympics into the confines of one small covered ice-arena.

Suddenly a tiny figure pushed her way through the athletes to clear a place for herself on the ice. With a quick jump into a sit-spin she signaled the beginning of her free-skate portion of the competition. Norwegian-born Sonja Henie, barely twelve years old, astonished spectators with her acrobatic agility. They had never seen a child in international competition before, and although her skating was far from polished and mature (she finished last), her technical skill and obvious determination were a delight to watch.

This was just the beginning of an unusual career that would span oceans and a half-century of world-wide fame. Although she came to glory on the ice, Ms. Henie was an all-around athlete. She won Scandinavian championships in tennis and skiing, and excelled in sprinting, swimming, and horseback riding. During her competitive figure-skating years, she won nearly fifteen hundred cups, medals, and trophies, including ten consecutive world titles and three Olympic gold medals in 1928, 1932, and 1936.

It is not Sonja Henie's victories that will

*Sonja Henie, winner of three Olympic medals in figure skating, was only ten years old when she won her first Norwegian national title in 1924.*
WIDE WORLD

be remembered, however, but rather her enormous success in Hollywood as the "golden girl" of the ice. In the heyday of the movies, Sonja starred in eleven extravagant Darryl F. Zanuck productions for 20th Century Fox. The lavish screenplays featuring the beautiful, dazzlingly costumed figure skater were seen by millions all over the world.

Sonja Henie popularized a sport that had been reserved for the very rich or for those living in countries where natural ice was common. Artificial-ice rinks began to spring up everywhere. It was not unusual to see new skaters industriously trying to imitate Ms. Henie's spectacular twists, turns, and spins. Dancing on ice became a common pastime. One of Sonja's films, *Sun Valley Serenade*, inspired Russia's Ludmila Beloussova to take up figure skating. Ludmila and her husband Oleg Protopopov were the winners of the 1964 and 1968 Olympic Pairs event. They had been called the most classical ice-skating pair the world had ever known.

In 1969, Sonja Henie died of leukemia when she was fifty-seven years old. She had amassed an estimated $47 million in the entertainment world. The sight of the whirling figure skater will live forever on the reels of celluloid that made this three-time Olympic gold medalist immortal.

*Movie-star Sonja Heine, shown here with Harrison Thomson in the Hollywood Ice Review, opened the era of the big-time ice spectaculars.*     UPI

# Of Blades and Scalpels

## • TENLEY ALBRIGHT

When Tenley Albright was only nine years old, in 1944, her first skating instructor, Willie Frick, said of her, "She's got it in the head and heart and that's why she can make it come out through her feet." The years ahead were to prove that Tenley would achieve success through her talented feet and through her skillful hands as well.

Tenley was a fortunate youngster — growing up in an affluent Boston home in which her successful surgeon father could afford to give her expensive figure-skating lessons. But as so many skaters have discovered, lessons alone do not make champions, and Tenley did have that extra something. She was a perfectionist, who loved to skate.

In figure skating, more than in any other sport, perhaps, tedious practice is an essential ingredient for championship form. Progress is recorded as the skater masters each of seventy school figures based on the tracing and retracing of two- and three-lobed figure eights. In less than three years after her first lesson, even after many months of inactivity because of a bout with polio, Tenley won her first title — the Eastern regional championship for juveniles under twelve. She followed it up with the national novice title when she was thirteen and the national junior championship a year later.

Now Tenley was ready for the majors. In 1952 she went to Oslo, Norway, as a member of the U.S. Olympic team. There she won a silver medal, the first for America since Beatrix Loughran won hers in 1924. The following year Tenley became this country's first winner of the world championship, and that along with the U.S. and North American titles made her America's first triple-crown figure skater.

An eighteen-year-old ice queen, Tenley then started on another career, that of becoming a doctor. In the fall of 1953, she entered prestigious Radcliffe College in Cambridge, Massachusetts. Combining school with ice-skating was not easy and in 1954, while defending her world title in Norway, the overworked co-ed fell on the ice, in the middle of a combination axel and double-loop jump. And so the queen lost her crown.

Perhaps another athlete with three na-

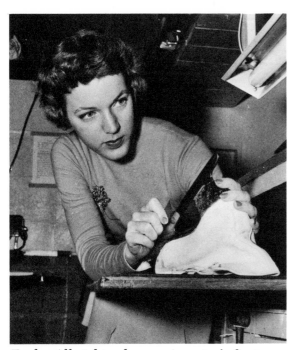

*Tenley Albright, who was America's first world chamion figure skater, went on to become a successful surgeon.*

*Nineteen-year-old Tenley Albright won her second world crown in 1955 and an Olympic gold medal the following year in Cortina, Italy.*

tional championships and a triple slam to her credit might have given up to devote all her attention to her studies. But Tenley was still a champion at heart, and with the help and encouragement of her coach, Maribel Vinson, she rescheduled her priorities with the primary goal the winning back of the world title. The pressure was intense. Tenley would get up when it was still dark and practice in a Boston arena from four to six in the morning, before classes. Then there were ballet lessons in addition to homework and study. It all added up to a grueling, exhausting schedule, but Tenley was confident that she was ready for the challenge.

At the Weiner Eislauf Verein Stadium in Vienna in 1955 Coach Vinson described the eventful week of the championships: "Tenley practiced on uneven ice . . . in sun, snow, and even rain. During the two days of competition, Tenley's lead increased with each figure she skated. In the end, a sparkling free-skating performance, this time without error of any kind, made her, by the unanimous verdict of the nine judges, champion of the world once more."

From there Tenley went on to the Winter Olympics in Cortina, Italy, in 1956, where she became the first American woman to win a gold medal in figure skating.

Somehow, through all this practice and time out for competition, Tenley's studies did not suffer. After only three years as an undergraduate, the twenty-one-year-old was accepted at Harvard Medical School, one of six women in a class of one hundred and thirty. With the same heart and determination that made her an ice champion, Tenley became a skilled and successful surgeon.

"One can't just go through life without giving back to it," she had once said. And there was no doubt that this talented athlete had indeed put her heart into her hands as well as her feet.

# Cutting Corners

## • CAROL HEISS

A complaint long registered to the United States Figure Skating Association is that figure skating is primarily a sport for the wealthy. Mrs. Sonya Fuhrman Allen, a former Swedish champion and mother of American ex-champion Scott Allen, once summed it up: "Figure skating is a luxury sport. If you can't afford it, don't get in it. I have seen many talented kids who couldn't get anywhere because they didn't have enough money."

Carol Heiss was a poor youngster, daughter of a struggling German-born baker. Yet she had the kind of parents who were willing to make the personal sacrifices required to make her a champion.

The family, including brother Bruce and sister Nancy, lived in a modest house in Ozone Park, New York. When Carol was five she got her first pair of skates and to everyone's amazement skated off with no difficulty and in perfect balance. Since there were no rinks near the Heiss home, Carol's mother took her pigtailed daughter by subway to the Brooklyn Ice Palace. There, the sight of the tiny darting youngster delighted everyone.

When she was six, Carol made her first public appearance in an amateur show put on by the Figure Skating Club of Brooklyn. Her first teacher, Ingrid Lordahl, was so impressed with the little girl's talent that she urged the Heisses to take her to Pierre and Andree Brunet, instructors at the Skating Club of New York, for lessons.

The Brunets would not take on any pupil who did not have unusual ability, nor anyone who was not prepared to devote long years to practice and competition. At the audition, Mr. and Mrs. Heiss, who realized how expensive a skating career would be, wanted to know just how far Carol could go. "In ten years," Pierre Brunet told them, "your daughter can be the best in the world." Carol and her parents accepted the challenge.

In the beginning, Carol had lessons twice a week. To earn the extra money needed, Mrs. Heiss took on free-lance jobs as a fabric designer. Since she would not let Carol travel alone in New York, she took her drawing board with her and worked on the designs while waiting at the New York Skating Club.

Now, too, Nancy and Bruce began to show promise on the ice, and their parents decided that the younger children should also have lessons. The three youngsters, known as "the golden kids," were a popular sight at the rink, working on routines together. Costs continued to mount. Coach Pierre suggested that Carol take piano lessons to improve her sense of rhythm, and ballet lessons to develop her style and balance. More expenses.

Mr. and Mrs. Heiss worked hard, cutting corners in every way possible. For years they paid for all of the children's expensive lessons and skates from their limited income. Mrs. Heiss and the girls designed and sewed all the skating costumes themselves.

When Carol was ten, she began to show her championship style. She won the Middle Atlantic and national junior titles. Now Mr. Brunet, aware of the financial burden on the Heiss family, suggested that they pay only what they could afford for his lessons. Still, the costly skates and transportation fares to competitive meets all over the country were a tremendous strain on the household.

Carol had difficulty keeping up with her school work. Traveling into New York every day for practice and lessons was too much for her. It was decided that she should go the the Professional Children's School in Manhattan, a public school attended by children in the performing arts. The school makes provisions for its pupils to continue their outside careers (with the odd hours of practice and performances) and still continue with their required schooling at whatever hours are convenient for them.

Carol worked doubly hard now. She knew how important it was to her parents that their struggles be rewarded. In 1953, when she was only thirteen, she went to Davos, Switzerland, to compete in the world championships. This was the year that Tenley Albright became America's first world champion. Carol came in fourth.

Carol would meet Tenley again six times

in the next three years. And always she would be the runner-up. In the 1956 Winter Olympics at Cortina, Italy, sixteen-year-old Carol was the youngest girl ever to skate for the United States. On one of Cortina's coldest days, the half-frozen teen-ager went down in defeat to Tenley Albright for the last time.

Two weeks later, Carol won the world crown in Garmisch, Germany, ending Tenley's reign. The hard-earned victory came none too soon. Shortly thereafter, Carol's mother died of cancer. Carol had promised Mrs. Heiss she would not give up amateur competition until she had won an Olympic gold medal. After first winning world championships four more years in a row, Carol kept her word. At Squaw Valley, California, in 1960, she became America's second figure-skating gold medalist.

John V. Lindsay, then a New York congressman, made a speech in Washington. "It is refreshing," he said, "to have someone like Carol Heiss set such high standards of courage and strength for our youth to follow." Carol and her family had proven that even in figure skating, you needn't be wealthy to make it to the top.

*Carol Heiss won the first of five world championships in 1956, when she was only sixteen years old.* WIDE WORLD

# A Break in the Ice

- **LAWRENCE OWEN**
- **MARIBEL OWEN**
- **MARIBEL VINSON-OWEN**

February 15, 1961, was a glorious, sunshiny day, with not a cloud in the sky. Six hundred feet above the Brussels Airport a Sabena Boeing 707 jet was circling, awaiting its turn to land. At ten in the morning the control tower signaled the hovering craft to give a taxiing plane time to clear the runway below.

In the air, eighteen members of the United States figure-skating team were eagerly anticipating the world championships in Prague. Hopes were high. In the group was sixteen-year-old Lawrence Owen, who three days earlier had become the North American women's champion and was the most likely candidate for a medal at the world meet. Her sister and fellow skater, Maribel, and their mother, Mrs. Maribel Vinson-Owen, ex-champion and coach, peered out of the small round window and watched anxiously as the huge plane veered away from the airport — north, toward the small farming community of Berg, barely 4 miles away.

Suddenly the engines gave an unexpected roar, the plane tipped to a 70-degree angle and, like a bird skipping a wing beat, began to lose altitude. A few peasants in the cabbage field below looked up toward the erratic noise and watched in horror as the jet suddenly began to plunge earthward, finally exploding in a mass of flaming, twisted metal.

No one had a chance. All seventy-three persons aboard the plane and a farmer died instantly. Gone were the lovely young athletes who had been filled with hope and promise. Gone were three members of the Vinson-Owen skating family.

Lawrence had been praised by *Sports Illustrated* after she placed sixth in the 1960 Olympic Games in Squaw Valley, California: "Her free-skating has an air, a style, an individuality which sets her apart from all the work done in recent years."

The youngster had her mother's drive and ability. After her success in the North American championships, she had been America's only genuine hope for the 1964 Olympics.

Mother Maribel, born in 1911, was the daughter of the late Thomas Vinson, also an accomplished skater. When Maribel was three years old, she put on her first pair of double-runner skates. Thirteen years later she took the national championship away from Theresa Weld, America's first and six-time winner of that title.

Maribel, a master at school figures, was a bold and daring skater. The slender, graceful girl won the national title a total of nine times and the pairs title six. She attained international prominence in the 1932 Olympics, when she came in third behind reigning queen Sonja Henie. She made headlines again in 1956 as the coach of America's first Olympic gold medalist in figure skating, Tenley Albright.

After the airplane accident, *The New York Times* mourned the tragedy on its editorial page: "There is a special feeling of loss and grief over the young athletes — and at the death of Mrs. Maribel Vinson-Owen, former writer of women's sports for *The New York Times*. Mrs. Owen and her two daughters and the other members of the U.S. figure skating team who perished were all skaters in the championship class."

*Renowned coach and nine-time national champion Maribel Vinson-Owen was killed in 1961 along with her two daughters and fifteen other members of the U.S. Olympic figure-skating team.*

UPI

# The Ballerina

## • PEGGY FLEMING

After the 1961 tragic airplane crash near Brussels, Belgium, took the lives of eighteen members of the United States figure skating team, the world was shocked and grieved. Pierre Brunet, coach of five-time world champion Carol Heiss, made a gloomy prediction. "Skating has received an incalculable setback," he said. "It will take a decade to make an American champion of international caliber. It's up to the fourteen- and fifteen-year-olds now."

Peggy Fleming was only thirteen when the accident occurred. She had already won the Pacific Coast juvenile and novice ladies' championships. Her coach, Billy Kipp, was killed in the crash, and Peggy keenly felt the loss. She was determined to honor his memory by doing her competitive best.

Early in 1964, when Peggy was fifteen, she became America's youngest national champion. Following that, she earned a berth on the U.S. Olympic team, and although considered a novice in international competition, she finished sixth at the Winter Olympics in Innsbruck, Austria. When she returned home, however,

her ego was quickly deflated by her classmates at Pasadena High in California. "What do you mean, you didn't bring home a medal?" they teased.

"I was just crushed," said Peggy, "but I think I really grew up as a result."

Her skating too, continued to ripen. In Davos, Switzerland, in 1966, only five years after the air crash, she won her first world championship and followed that with a victorious tour of England, Austria, Germany, Russia, and France. In 1967, after making a clean sweep on the ice — winning the North American, world, and national titles — she headed for the Winter Games in Grenoble, France.

On Saturday, February 10, 1968, millions of people around the world were glued to their television sets. The marvels of the space age enabled the ABC-TV network to televise the tenth Winter Olympiad live via satellite to all parts of the globe. Forty cameras fed into twenty-one monitors at the huge TV control center.

In the Stade de Glace Peggy nervously awaited her turn at the free-skating performance. In the days past she had piled up an impressive, almost unbeatable, 77.2

*Star of her own TV special, Peggy Fleming won America's only gold medal at the 1968 Winter Olympics in Grenoble, France.*

point lead in the school figures. At last the slender 105-pound beauty in a chartreuse chiffon dress glided slowly onto the ice.

The powerful opening bars of Tchaikovsky's *Pathetique* signaled the start and Peggy was off with two double loops and a double axel. Her skating was mature and full of depth. She floated across the ice like a prima ballerina, effortlessly, with inspired grace. After a minute or two, the music changed to the melodious Romeo and Juliet *Overture* — a spreadeagle here, a double axel there. Another change of music and mood, this time to Saint-Saen's opera *Samson and Delilah*. Always smooth, always fluid, Peggy was pure dancer.

When it was all over, Peggy had won a gold medal, the only one for the United States in the 1968 Winter Games. To this she added her third world championship before announcing her retirement from amateur competition. A five-time national champion, Peggy was besieged with extravagant offers. In April, 1968, she accepted an estimated $500,000 contract, which called for her appearance in TV and ice-show spectaculars. For years to come, millions of spectators would continue to thrill at the sight of the ballerina on ice.

# Million-Dollar Baby

## • JANET LYNN

Shy, chubby Janet Lynn Nowicki clung desperately to her father's jacket. This was at her brother's Cub Scout outing on a pond in southwest Chicago, and two-and-a-half-year-old Janet was wearing her first pair of ice skates.

With every step on the tiny blades, the roly-poly toddler would fall. Still, she was having a wonderful time; always laughing, pulling herself up over and over again, never crying for help. To everyone's amazement, by the end of the afternoon, Janet had taught herself to skate backwards. The little girl was so delighted with her new skill that the Nowickis decided to put her in a skating class instead of continuing her in dancing school. She had been so painfully shy in dance class that she had to be forced to get out on the exercise floor.

In skating school, she needed no urging. By the time she was four, Janet had advanced beyond the teacher and everyone else in school. In 1961, Mr. and Mrs. Nowicki, realizing that their youngster had an extraordinary talent, moved the family closer to good ice and more professional coaching.

Their new home was in Rockford, Illinois, just 14 miles from the Wagon Wheel resort, famous for its ice rink and skating pro Slavka Kohout. The Kohout-Nowicki team were a brilliant teacher-student combination, and before long there emerged from the Wagon Wheel Ice Palace a new star — now known simply as Janet Lynn — a petite, graceful and talented competitor.

Janet's success was phenomenal. At seven, in her first competition, the Midwestern juvenile ladies, she finished thirteenth. The following year, she became the Upper Great Lakes novice champion, and when she was twelve she won the national junior title. She was only thirteen when she finished fourth in the senior ladies competition, and in 1968, when she was fourteen, she made the U.S. Olympic team. The next year, she won her first national championship and did so again for four more consecutive years. In 1972, Janet Lynn won an Olympic bronze medal in Sapporo, Japan, and a year later came in second to Canada's Karen Magnussen in the World Championships at Bratislava, Czechoslovakia.

But competitive skating was an exhausting, expensive, and pressure-ridden life, and after fourteen years of hard work and social isolation, Janet was ready to make a change. She was twenty-one-years-old. She had always had a simple, almost evangelical faith in God, and now she sought his guidance. When she was offered a three-year contract for $1.4 million with the Shipstads and Johnson Ice Follies, she said that God had given her the answer. "I believe," she said, "that God has given me this contract as a gift . . . one I can use as I wish . . . to help others."

And so it was that this beautiful, talented ice queen started out on a new road. Between travels with her ice show, she addressed civic and social groups, visited hospitals and churches, and generously promoted charitable causes all across the country.

At the time Janet Lynn's million-dollar-plus contract made her the highest paid woman athlete in America. To Janet, her million may have been God's gift, but to women athletes everywhere, it was a much needed boost in the continuing battle for professional equality with men.

*Janet Lynn, who was a national champion five times, signed a $1.4 million contract with the Shipstads and Johnson Ice Follies in 1973.*

UPI

# An American Beauty Rose

## • DOROTHY HAMILL

She came to Innsbruck, Austria, for the 1976 Winter Olympics boasting relatively few headlines in the course of her eight-year figure skating career. She had been the U.S. title-holder in 1974 and 1975, but nineteen-year-old Dorothy Hamill was still relatively unknown to the public. She had not achieved the fame and popularity of such earlier champions as Carol Heiss, Peggy Fleming, or Janet Lynn. Yet the experts predicted that the athletic Ms. Hamill might win a medal — and certainly she was America's best hope.

Dorothy, who grew up in Riverside, Connecticut, had trained in Denver, Colorado, since 1973 under Carlo Fassi, Peggy Fleming's coach. "They are quite different in many ways." the coach had said. "Dorothy is better on spins and is more powerful and athletic. Peggy is more of the ballet school."

The favorites at Innsbruck were Dianne de Leeuw of the Netherlands, who had defeated Dorothy in the world championships in 1975, and East Germany's Christine Errath, the 1974 world titlist.

On the first day of competition, Dorothy took an early lead in the three compulsory figures. Scoring in figure skating is done in three areas: compulsory figures in which a skater must trace three figures drawn from a hat by the judges; a two-minute short program made up of seven well-rehearsed compulsory moves; and a four-minute free-skating program in which the skaters can do anything. The compulsory figures and free-skating count 30 and 50 percent respectively, and the short program 20 percent.

Dorothy moved still further ahead in the two-minute compulsories by posting a perfect score of 6 for technical merit and artistic expression. By the last day of competition, it became apparent that Dorothy had a good chance to win it all.

Her four-minute free-skating program was fourteenth in the line-up. Wearing an American Beauty rose costume, Dorothy performed brilliantly to the music taped by her business-executive father, Chalmers. Melodies from an old Errol Flynn movie, *Seahawk*, provided the background for her almost flawless execution of jumps, spins, splits, and flying leaps. The 5 foot 3 inch skater made an impressive exit doing her signature move, a "Hamill camel" (a spin into a sitspin).

Now the music was replaced by pro-

*Dorothy Hamill defeated 1975 world champion Dianne de Leeuw to win the Olympic gold medal in Innsbruck, Austria, in 1976.*   UPI

longed, vociferous cheering from the packed ice arena. The scores of the nine judges flashed on the electric scoreboard — eight 5.8s and a 5.9 for technical merit, a row of 5.9s for artistic expression.

When Ms. de Leeuw, the last of the twenty competitors, had completed her free-skating program, it was evident that Dorothy Hamill had won the gold medal. This American beauty, who did most things left-handed, had surely and effectively skated right.

# SPEED SKATING

## The Girls of the Silver Skates

- **JENNIFER FISH**
- **ANNE HENNING**
- **DIANNE HOLUM**
- **MARY MEYERS**
- **SHEILA YOUNG**

The ice of the Parc Paul Mistral skating rink in Grenoble, France, was getting soft as the temperature soared well above freezing. It was February 9, 1968, the day of the women's 500-meter speed skating event at the Winter Olympic Games. There were twenty-eight women competing against the clock, among them Jennifer Fish, Dianne Holum, and Mary Meyers from the United States.

When it was Mary's turn, she breezed around the course in what seemed to be excellent time, 46.3 seconds. Dianne, also fast, crossed the finish line with the official stopwatch reading 46.3 seconds. Finally, when Jenny flashed around the track and the electronic clock once again stopped exactly at 46.3 seconds, the crowd knew it had witnessed a most unusual tie. After all the times had been recorded, the U.S.

*From left to right: Jennifer Fish, Mary Meyers, and Dianne Holum, who tied for the silver medal in 500-meter speed skating, with Russian gold medalist Ludmila Titova at the 1968 Winter Olympics in Grenoble, France.*

UPI

In 1971 Anne Henning won the Women's World Championship 500-meter event at Helsinki.                                    UPI

Sheila Young, first American triple-medalist in the Winter Games at Innsbruck in 1976.
                                    WIDE WORLD

girls of the silver skates were found to have won three silver medals. It was the best American women had ever done in Olympic speed skating competition and they had come in only two-tenths of a second behind the winner, Russia's Ludmilla Titova. Before the events at Grenoble closed, Dianne had also won a bronze in the 1000 meters, with Ludmilla taking the silver and Carolina Geijssen of the Netherlands the gold.

Speed skating for women first became an Olympic event in 1960 at Squaw Valley, California, and that year Jeanne Ashworth, a twenty-one-year-old Tufts University co-ed from Wilmington, Massachusetts, won third place in the 500-meter race. However, the 1932 Winter Olympics at Lake Placid, New York, did include demonstration races on the program and Americans Elizabeth Dubois and Kit Klein were winners of the 500- and 1000-meter exhibition events, respectively.

After the unforgettable triple tie in 1968, sixteen-year-old Dianne Holum returned to her home in Northbrook, Illinois. The park commissioner of Northbrook, an affluent suburb of Chicago, was a speed-skating enthusiast named Big Ed Rudolph. He was responsible for the formation of the Northbrook Speed Skating Club, a group that had gained a reputation for training superior competitive skaters. When Dianne qualified for the 1972 Olympic team she was joined in Sapporo, Japan, by another Northbrook resident, sixteen-year-old Anne Henning. This time the American skaters won two gold medals — Dianne at 1500 meters, Anne in the 500.

By 1975, Northbrook was appropriately known as the "Speed Capital of the World." It had trained twenty-nine national champions, eight world team members, and ten Olympic team members, of which eight were women.

It was a girl from Detroit, however, who gave the most remarkable performance in 1976, at Innsbruck, Austria. Sheila Young, also a champion cyclist, showed her strength and speed on ice when she became the first American triple-medalist in the Winter Olympic Games. Sheila won a gold medal in the 500-meter event, silver in the 1500, and bronze in the 1000.

After she achieved her third medal, President Ford called Innsbruck to congratulate her, but Sheila was touring the countryside. When she called back, the White House would not accept the collect call. After a brief explanation, the connection was made. Sheila had brought honor to her home state of Michigan (President Ford's too), and the nation as well.

# GOLF
## Trailblazer on the Green

### • GLENNA COLLETT

In 1903, when Glenna Collett was born, a sports writer of the time had this to say about lady golfers: "The women swing at the ball as though they were beating off purse-snatchers with an umbrella."

The emergence of Ms. Collett changed all that. When Glenna was six years old, her family moved to Providence, Rhode Island, where her father, an expert golfer, joined the Metacomet Golf Club. Glenna, a tomboy at heart, was reputed to have driven an automobile when she was ten. Soon the little girl was joining her dad at the club, and because of her natural ability she was allowed to play the course. When she was seventeen she entered major competition.

Glenna's career was unequaled in the annals of golf. She won the National Amateur golf championship a record six times, and was known as the Bobby Jones of women's golf. Champion Jones said this of Glenna: "It is especially a treat to watch Glenna Collett. Her accuracy with the spoon and brassie [commonly used clubs] is to me the most important part of her well-rounded game. It is, of course, her way of absorbing to a great extent, the disadvantage of length, which some women suffer against the best males; but she does it with little disadvantage to be noticed."

In 1935, five years after winning her fifth National title, Glenna, who had become Mrs. Edwin Vare, appeared at the Interlachen Country Club of Minneapolis. After a two-year retirement to have two children, she was competing again in the National Amateur. The final day of the tournament was cold, rainy, and miserable, but an unprecedented gallery of 15,000 spectators turned out to watch. Glenna was competing against some of the best young players — Marian McDougal, twenty-one; Marian Miley, twenty-one; Betty Jameson, seventeen; and Patty Berg, seventeen. Thirty-two-year-old Mrs. Vare had to do some fancy swinging to recapture the title. And she did!

Bernard Swanson, sports editor of the Minneapolis *Star*, paid her a glowing tribute. "It isn't everyone," he wrote, "who, playing in their fourteenth national championship is still good enough to cope with the next generation. And fewer still could win."

And as if that victory weren't enough, this grand dame of golf won the Rhode Island state championship when she was fifty-six years old — thirty-seven years after winning it for the first time in 1922!

*Glena Collett, one of America's early golfers, won the National title a record six times—the first in 1922, and the last thirteen years later in 1935.*

# Linking the Years

## • PATTY BERG

The snub-nosed, freckle-faced youngster was heartbroken. Her parents insisted that she stop playing football with the boys. "You're a big girl now," they'd said.

Fourteen-year-old Patricia Ann Berg had always played with the boys. In fact, she was among the first chosen when sides were picked for all the neighborhood teams. She was a great athlete, as the guys knew, but they also admired her for her sense of fair play and sportsmanship and had even asked her to be their coach.

Now, her ball-playing days were over, and Patty was in search of another sport to challenge her.

"How about golf?" her father had asked, and since the Minneapolis golf links were only a few miles from the Bergs' home, Patty decided to give it a try. She rounded up a makeshift set of clubs — three old brassies, three irons, and a putter — from her dad and hitched a ride to the course. It took her 112 strokes to get around the 18 holes that day in 1932, but when this natural athlete returned six years later, she scored a 70, playing from the men's tees!

The Berg family joined the Interlachen Country Club so Patty would have a place to practice, and her determination and unusual talent soon added up to a superior golfer. She qualified in less than a year for the Minnesota State championships, starting a record in which she qualified for every tournament she ever entered. By the time Patty was twenty in 1938 and had won the National Amateur title in Wilmette, Illinois, she was considered the foremost woman golfer in the United States. Before leaving amateur golf to turn pro, she was selected the Woman Athlete of the Year by the Associated Press three times, had won forty tournaments, and played twice on the Curtis Cup team with Glenna Collett.

In 1940 Ms. Berg became one of the first amateurs to turn pro and started on the second phase of her extraordinary career. She helped organize the Ladies Professional Golf Association (LPGA) in 1948 and served as its president for the next four years. She is credited with having done more for the establishment of women's professional golf than anyone else in the game.

Four decades after giving up football

*Patty Berg was seventeen here, when she reached the finals of the National Women's Golf Championships in 1935. She won the event three years later.*

UPI

with the boys, Patty Berg was still hitting a golf ball with the power of most men. She had been victorious in eighty-one tournaments including the first National Open in 1946. She won the Titleholders (women's Masters) seven times; the World Championship at Tom O'Shanter four times; and the Vare Trophy, given to the woman scoring the lowest annual average, three times. The enduring Ms. Berg shot a 64 in the Richmond Open at Richmond, California, in 1952, which stood as the LPGA 18-hole scoring record for twelve years and even today is hard to beat.

In 1941, just after Patty turned pro, her first prize money for winning the U.S. Women's Open was a $100 bond. In spite of this humble beginning, Patty was among the first of the lady golfers to make money on the circuit. She was leading money winner of the LPGA three times, averaging over $16,000 in prize money each year. In 1951 she was honored by being elected to the LPGA Hall of Fame.

Patty Berg was still playing championship golf in 1975, when she entered the Dinah Shore Open in Palm Springs, California. And she still held her record for qualifying in every tournament she had ever entered.

43

# The Babe

## • MILDRED DIDRIKSON ZAHARIAS

When the Associated Press polled the nation's sports writers in 1950 to choose the Woman Athlete of the Half-Century, there was little doubt as to the outcome. Babe Didrikson Zaharias was chosen almost unanimously. The noted author Paul Gallico went even further in his acclaim: "She was probably the most talented athlete, male or female, ever developed in our country. In all my years at the sports desk I never encountered any man who could play as many different games as well as the Babe."

Babe Didrikson had a spectacular career: as a basketball star, an Olympic gold medalist in track and field, and a national and international champion in amateur and professional golf. She also excelled in every other sport she tried and could probably have become a champion in any one of them had she chosen to. She could swim, dive, play tennis, ride a horse, ice-skate, shoot billiards, bowl in the 200's, pitch, and belt a baseball.

And if the Babe could play games as well as many men, she could also sew better, cook better, and type better than most women. Although she was considered the perpetual tomboy, she was also a warm, outgoing woman with many feminine interests. "I was always determined to be the greatest athlete that ever lived," she said in her autobiography, *This Life I've Led*. "But I loved pretty things around the house, too."

Both the rugged and domestic qualities of the Babe were developed early, in the loving, close-knit circle of family life. She was born in 1914 Mildred Ella Didrikson, sixth in a family of seven children. Mr. and Mrs. Didrikson were Norwegian immigrants who had to work hard to make a good life for their large family. Mr. Didrikson was an avid sports fan, and since he could not afford to buy elaborate sports equipment for his growing family, he found other ways to encourage physical activity. In the backyard he set up a gym with broom-handle bars for jumping and hurdling. In the garage he made a barbell from another handle with flatirons at either end for weightlifting. Babe proved early what a natural athlete she was, and during her last years at Beaumont (Texas) High School was the team's star basketball player.

As the only member of the Employers Casualty Company track team competing at the tryouts for the 1932 Olympic Games, super athlete Babe Didrikson won six of the eight events she entered.          UPI

Although not much over five feet at the time, the amazing Babe won two gold medals and a silver in the three events she was allowed to enter at the 1932 Olympics.          WIDE WORLD

The Texas newspapers were filled with stories about her skill on the court, and this came to the attention of Colonel M. J. McCombs, director of the women's athletic program at Employers Casualty Company. After her graduation, the Babe was asked to join the company's basketball team, and to set up a track squad as well.

At the Amateur Athletic Union tryouts for the Olympic team in 1932, she was the sole entry from Employers Casualty. Of the eight events the Babe entered, she placed in seven, including six firsts. Single-handedly, she won the championship for Employers Casualty and a berth on the U.S. Olympic team. Eighteen-year-old Mildred Didrikson was soon on her way to Los Angeles, site of the summer Olympics.

This time, the Babe was allowed to enter only three events. Still not much over 5 feet tall, and weighing only 105 pounds, this versatile young competitor won two gold medals and a silver, breaking her own world record in both the javelin (143 feet 4 inches) and the 80-meter hurdles (11.7 seconds). She might have won the high jump too, but placed second to Jean Shiley because of a peculiarity in her style of jumping, which disqualified her final record jump.

In the press box afterwards, famous sports writer Grantland Rice invited the all-around athlete to a round of golf at the Broadmore Country Club. It would be the first time Babe would play in a formal 18-hole match. After playing with her, Granny Rice, who had watched all of the great golfers of his time, wrote that he'd never seen a woman hit a golf ball that way. He predicted that she would soon be a champion golfer.

With grit, determination, and long hours of practice in addition to her natural talents, Babe Didrikson did become one of the world's greatest golfers. After taking time out to earn some money in athletic exhibitions and a vaudeville act at the Palace Theater in Chicago, she won her first amateur golf tournament, the Fort

Worth Invitational, in 1935. Two days later, she was declared ineligible as an amateur because of the money she had earned as an athlete.

She joined golfer Gene Sarazen on the professional circuit and continued to play exhibition golf. She regularly drove shots 300 yards and once stroked a ball an amazing 346 yards! In 1938, when she was twenty-three years old, she met wrestler George Zaharias while playing the Los Angeles Open, and before the year was out they were married.

In 1943 the Babe was reinstated as an amateur and her string of golf victories began piling up. She won such major tournaments as the U.S. Women's Amateur (1946), the British Women's Amateur (first for an American, 1947) and the U.S. Women's Open (1948, 1950, 1954). Over the 1946–47 seasons she set an all-time record by winning seventeen major tournaments in a row!

At the height of her career, in 1953, when she was only thirty-nine years old, Babe discovered she had cancer. Gifts and letters of encouragement poured in from all over the world as she recuperated from a colostomy operation. With her golf clubs standing in the corner of her hospital room, and supported by her devoted husband, she was determined to get back on the golf course.

Just three-and-a-half months after she was wheeled into the operating room, the Babe was back in action, playing at Tam O'Shanter in the All-American tournament. She placed fifteenth. Two days later, she played the same course again, this time coming in third for the World Championship. Yet, this was not good enough for the Babe. Despite the pain and exhaustion, she continued to work for her old top position. "One reason I don't re-

*Mildred "Babe" Didrikson, named "Babe" after the mighty home-run hitter Babe Ruth, once threw a baseball 296 feet.*

WIDE WORLD

*During the 1946-47 season, Mrs. Babe Didrikson Zaharias won seventeen golf tournaments in a row.*                                                                    UPI

tire," she said, "is that every time I get out and play well in a tournament, it seems to encourage people with the same trouble I had." She was honored with the Ben Hogan Trophy for the Greatest Comeback of the Year.

The following year, 1954, she really came back to full glory. She won the U.S. Women's Open by a record lead of 12 strokes and returned to Tam O'Shanter to win the All-American. For the fifth time

she was voted Woman Athlete of the Year. She told the world, "This should show people not to be afraid of cancer. I'll go on golfing for years."

But that did not happen. Babe Didrikson Zaharias, champion until the end, died on September 27, 1956. She will always be remembered for her optimism, honesty, warmth, and courage. She was America's greatest woman athlete, and an even greater human being.

# Swingers on the Fairway

- CAROL MANN
- SANDRA PALMER
- BETSY RAWLS
- KATHY WHITWORTH
- MICKEY WRIGHT

It took a dozen years for Patty Berg's LPGA (Ladies Professional Golf Association) 18-hole scoring record of 64 to be broken. Mickey Wright, a statuesque Californian, did it in 1964 with a score of 62 on the Hogan Park course in Midland, Texas.

When superstar Babe Didrikson saw Mickey play in her first Women's Open tournament ten years earlier, she watched in amazement as the nineteen-year-old swung her way around the course.

"Gee whiz, get a load of that," Babe said to her husband, George Zaharias. "I didn't think anyone but the Babe could hit 'em like that. If I'm around five years from now, I'll have my hands full." Sadly, the incomparable Babe was not around that long. She died in 1956 and 5 foot 9 inch Mickey took her place as the "new Babe."

Mickey was already 5 feet 8 inches when she celebrated her eleventh birthday in 1946. Her dad gave her the first set of clubs as a present — a wood, two irons, and a putter — and Mickey promptly broke all four in the backyard during her first day of swinging at the ball. She played on a regulation course from then on.

At twelve, she was scoring 100; at thirteen, in the high 80's. At fourteen, Mickey won her first tournament, the Southern California Girl's Championship. The following year, at the Invitational Tournament at La Jolla, California, she made her first hole-in-one and won the event. Mickey rounded out her amateur career in 1954 by winning the All-American and world crowns. She then made the difficult decision to discontinue her studies at Stanford University in order to turn professional.

Mickey ushered in a new era in women's golf. She was to exemplify a whole breed of exciting personalities in the sport. The professional lady golfers finally began to draw large galleries to their tournaments. But it was a tough road to travel. While the men were winning as much as $50,000 for a single tournament, the women were looked upon with contempt. Their game was considered to be either "powder puff" in quality, or "Amazonian." The girls had to play superior golf, and were also required to have personality, good looks, and charm.

Mickey drew the crowds. She played tremendous golf, often outdistancing her

Mickey Wright won the grand slam of women's golf in 1961: the Titleholders, the U.S. Open, and the Ladies Professional Golf Association Championship.      UPI

rivals by as much as 50 yards off the tee. In 1961, she won the grand slam of women's golf: the Titleholders, the Open, and the LPGA Championship. She was named Woman Athlete of the Year in 1963 and 1964. For five consecutive years Mickey was leading money-winner on the tour, averaging over $26,000 annually in prize money. When the thirty-year-old champion decided to retire from the tournament trail to resume her studies at Southern Methodist University, everyone thought the tour would fall apart.

Kathy Whitworth, Mickey's chief rival on the circuit, observed: "Suddenly the top is gone. Even if I do turn out to be number one, it won't taste the same. Everybody is going to say, 'Mickey Wright wasn't playing.' "

But Kathy was wrong. The galleries continued to grow — and now they came to see her. She was ranked first, and in 1965 won eight championships. She won the

Vare Trophy in 1969 for her low-scoring average of 72.61 and by 1975, after winning Colgate's Triple Crown tournament, Kathy headed the list of all-time career earnings with a whopping $555,343.

Betsy Rawls, the oldest and perhaps wisest of the circuit players (she was a Phi Beta Kappa from the University of Texas), was another drawing card. Betsy, who had won the Open four times, a record she shared with Mickey Wright, had been the leading money-winner twice and was elected to the Hall of Fame in 1960.

Perhaps the most exciting personality of all, however, was 6 foot 3 inch Carol Mann, an effervescent blonde from Buffalo, New York. Lennie Wirtz, the women's tour director said: "Once you meet her, you never forget her."

Carol was self-conscious about her height, but she was the pace-setter among fashionable women golfers. She was one of the few women to wear culottes on the

*After Kathy Whitworth won the Colgate Triple Crown Tournament in 1975, she headed the women's list of all-time career earners with a total of $555,343.*    UPI

*In addition to showing championship form on the golf course, statuesque Carol Mann brought stylish culottes and miniskirts to the green.*    WIDE WORLD

tour, and was always particularly careful to look as feminine as possible. "We should all try to look more ladylike on the course," she said. "Being thought of as anything but a woman absolutely frosts me." Carol won the Open in 1965 and, in a brilliant two-year streak, eighteen more tournaments. In 1969 she became the first woman to earn over $50,000 on the LPGA tour in one year.

In spite of this, however, the money earnings of women golfers nowhere approached the prize monies awarded to the men. Women's golf still needed a boost. It finally came from such commercial sponsors as Colgate, S & H Green Stamps, Sealy-Fabergé, and Sears. These companies, recognizing the power and skill of veteran golfers, and the appeal of such younger players as Jane Blalock, JoAnn Prentice, Judy Rankin, Sandra Haynie, and Sandra Palmer, offered new highs in prize monies.

Five foot one-and-a-half inch Sandra Palmer, winner of the U.S. Open in 1975, took home $32,000 for her one-shot victory over Kathy McMullen in Colgate's Winner Circle tournament that year. At long last, the champions of the fairway were swinging into the big time.

# Golden Girl of Golf

## • LAURA BAUGH

The beautiful blond sixteen-year-old would not give up. Although she had just lost the 1971 U.S. Girls' Amateur golf tournament, Laura Baugh was determined to try for the Women's Amateur title in Mobile, Alabama, less than a week away.

After hitting over a thousand balls till her hands were actually cracked and bleeding, the persevering youngster decided she had practiced enough. It was not considered likely that anyone so young would have a chance against the field of ninety-nine of the nation's most skilled and experienced golfers. Yet she surprised everyone by winning the title. Teen-ager Laura Baugh became the youngest U.S. Women's Amateur golf champion in history!

Florida-born Laura had been playing the game since she was two, when her father, Hale, put a club in her hands. Mr. Baugh, an ardent and expert golfer, had played on the University of Florida team and taught Laura all he knew about competitive golf. By the time she entered competition, she had developed a sophistication and maturity in play that gave her an advantage over most other golfers in her age group.

Starting in 1962, when she was seven, Laura won the Peewee championships and the Juniors many times. When she was fourteen and living in California with her divorced mother, she triumphed in the Los Angeles and Long Beach tournaments. She played like a woman; was truly master of her clubs — tee shots, fairway woods and irons, the wedge, and putting. She could lace the ball dead straight on the fairway for 215 yards or more!

After winning the U.S. Women's Amateur, Laura was forced by lack of finances to turn pro in the summer of 1973. "I couldn't afford to be an amateur, and I wanted to be self-supporting," she said. Her beauty and style made her a natural draw for the pro circuit. That year she was named Rookie Golfer of the Year and in the first eight events of the season collected $19,656 in winnings.

Having a lovely, shining face and perfect 5 foot 5 inch, 115-pound figure, Laura endorsed Wilson golf equipment, Ford Motor cars, Suzuki motorcycles, Rolex watches, Colgate's household products, a Bermuda tourist bureau, and two golf resorts. In addition, she served as a fashion consultant for the *Ladies Home Journal* and modeled sportswear for *Golf Magazine*.

Laura Baugh had earned a reputation as golf's Golden Girl; her enormous following was known as Laura's Legions. She served as an inspiration to young golfers everywhere who had once thought that golf was a sport for older, wealthy women. Laura's skill and diligence had enabled her to be self-supporting at the age of eighteen.

*When lovely Laura Baugh turned pro at eighteen, she wound up endorsing Wilson golf equipment, Ford Motor cars, Suzuki motorcycles, Rolex watches, and Colgate's household products.*

# GYMNASTICS

## Girls on the Beam

- **MURIEL DAVIS GROSSFELD**
- **LINDA METHENY**
- **CATHY RIGBY**

Although gymnastics had ranked as a major sport in Europe for several hundred years, it was a relatively minor one in America until TV cameras showed the grace and beauty of Olga Korbut, Linda Metheny, and Cathy Rigby in the 1970s.

Linda and Cathy's coach in the 1972 Olympics was veteran gymnast Muriel Davis Grossfeld, who first appeared on the vaulting horse and parallel bars in the 1956 Olympics in Melbourne, Australia. Muriel, who married Olympic gymnast champion Abe Grossfeld, was All-Around national titlist in 1957 and 1963; all told she took sixteen national victories in individual events starting in 1955. Ms. Grossfeld went on to coach the United States' Olympic and Pan-American teams from 1967 through 1972 and was on the scene when Linda Metheny and Cathy Rigby moved into the limelight.

Linda, who was described in the official 1972 U.S. Olympic Book as "the most dependable gymnast the U.S.A. ever had," was a five-time winner of the All-Around national championship. In the 1967 Pan-American Games in Winnipeg, Canada, she won a record five gold medals, and in

recognition of this feat was invited to carry the "colors" four years later in the opening ceremonies at the Pan-American Games in Cali, Colombia. As a three-time Olympian, Linda's most significant performance was in 1968 in Mexico City, when she came in fourth in the balance-beam competition and became the first American woman ever to qualify for the finals in an individual gymnastic event.

When ABC's Wide World of Sports televised eighteen-year-old Cathy Rigby winning her silver medal in the World Gymnastic championships in Yugoslavia in 1970, the world had its first view of an American woman taking an important place in international competition.

Cathy, born two months prematurely with collapsed lungs, weighed less than four pounds at her birth in 1952 in Los Alamitos, California. For the first five years, this frail child was in and out of hospitals, suffering from colds, fevers, pneumonia, and bronchitis.

Cathy's mother, who had been a victim of polio and could not walk without the aid of crutches, was a constant source of inspiration to her five children. Under her

*In the course of her competitive career, Olympic coach Muriel Davis Grossfeld won sixteen national victories in individual gymnastic events.* UPI

*Always dependable, Linda Jo Metheny was a five-time winner of the all-around national gymnastic title.* UPI

supervision, Cathy grew into a healthy, active, fearless youngster — throwing herself with gusto into every physical activity. When she was eight she discovered the delights of a trampoline at the local youth center. At her first class she was able to do back flips.

As the years progressed, the instructor was so impressed with Cathy's natural ability, he suggested the Rigbys take her to

SCAT (Southern California Acrobatic Team), a newly formed girl's gymnastic club under the direction of former Olympian Bud Marquette.

For the next five years, Cathy devoted herself exclusively to gymnastics and under Marquette's expert guidance soon developed into a first-class competitor. In 1968, when she was fifteen, she went to Mexico City with the Olympic team.

Many who saw her in Olympic Village that fall could not believe she was a competing athlete. The 4 foot 10 inch, 89-pound teen-ager, who wore a size 3 junior petit, seemed more like a team mascot. But Cathy soon proved she was a seasoned competitor when she placed sixteenth in the All-Around scoring. This was the highest Olympic position ever achieved by an American gymnast. By the time she competed in Munich in 1972, she was able to place tenth over-all, against the spectacular performances of the Russians, including Olga Korbut.

When Cathy retired from competition after the '72 Olympics, she turned to a career on the stage. Her first professional part was that of Peter Pan in a grandly extravagant show produced by the NBC Entertainment Corporation, which toured the United States and Europe. Although this skilled and dedicated gymnast would no longer appear in competition, flying fast behind her were rising amateurs Roxanne Pierce and Joan Moore Rice. Grown-up Cathy Rigby Mason (she married a professional football player) had led the way into what had once been a Never-Never-Land for American gymnasts.

*Cathy Rigby brought America it's first medal in international gymnastic competition when she won a silver at the 1970 World Championships in Yugoslavia.*

# The Pixie Who Bewitched the World

## • OLGA KORBUT

In the early 1970s, against a backdrop of such heavy political utterances as "iron curtain," "cold war," and "detente," there emerged from the Soviet Union a lightweight gymnast — 84-pound Olga Korbut. The 4 foot 10 inch teen-ager, with the pixielike grin and ribbons in her hair, bridged the gap between nations with her gaiety, youth, and tremendous talent. When she was seen from Russia via satellite on television in April, 1975, receiving Gilette's Cavalcade of Sports Award, people around the world applauded.

Olga was born in 1955 in the small city of Grodno in the Belorussian Republic. In all states of the Soviet Union, youngsters who showed unusual athletic promise were sent to regular academic school and to a special one for sports. Although Olga had the lowest marks in her class, she was better than most of the boys and girls of her age in physical education, so she was invited to attend a gymnastic school headed by coach Renald Knysh.

In gymnastic circles trainer Knysh's ideas were considered quite revolutionary. "Gymnastics is acrobatics on an apparatus," he said. "Everything done on the mat on the floor can be done on the parallel bars, on the balance beam, on the vaulting horse."

Knysh's pupils were taught to be fearless. He turned them into daredevils by inventing safety devices to help eliminate their fears. There was felt matting and padding everywhere in the gynasium . . . around all the poles in the apparatus, and in many layers on the floor.

Olga soon became one of Knysh's prize athletes. He worked with her incessantly. Although such stunts as a backward somersault on the 10-centimeter balance beam had always been considered impossible, Olga was able to perform it spectacularly in the Soviet championships in 1969. In 1972, she proudly joined the other 9,000 athletes from around the world at the Olympic Games in Munich, Germany.

For gymnastic competition the elements performed are divided into A, B, and C categories, depending on the degree of difficulty. Most gymnasts choose a well-balanced program including a few maneuvers from each of the divisions. Not Olga. By the time the competition was over, a special designation — "ultra-

C" — had been made up to accommodate the level of difficulty of her stunts. They came to be known as the "Korbut elements."

On the first day of competition, Olga and her teammates were given what seemed to be a sure team victory score of 9.75. Olga performed exquisitely — somersaults, pirouettes. The crowd saw her as a "grasshopper," a "butterfly," a "sparrow." The next day, however, still doing her ultra-C elements with spectacular perfection, she somehow blundered while doing the most simple A movements. When her individual, negligible score of 7.5 was announced, the seventeen-year-old burst into tears. She had obviously lost her chance for the combined first place victory. The 12,000 spectators in the packed stands of the Sporthalle Stadium reached out to her in a unified feeling of sympathy, warmth, and affection.

The applause was deafening when Olga returned to the floor to complete her part of the competition. To come back after having fallen so low was the mark of a truly mature athlete. After the final day's scoring had been tallied, young Olga had come in seventh, with teammate Ludmilla Tourishcheva first, East Germany's Karen Janz second, and Russia's Tamara Lazakovich third. The crowd, however, still considered little Olga the true queen.

As a team, the spectacular Soviet girls won the combined competition. In addition to the team gold medal, Olga took home two more golds and a silver in individual events. The Munich newspaper *Sportkurier* recorded the happenings: "The smallest girl was at the same time the greatest. In the finale, in the individual events, Olga Korbut was the worthiest recipient of the first place. . . ."

The Associated Press named the tiny gymnast Woman Athlete of the Year — twenty votes ahead of United States tennis star Billie Jean King. Olga was the first athlete from a Communist nation to receive this award. She was also honored with the Babe Didrikson Zaharias Trophy and was chosen ABC's Wide World of Sports 1972 Athlete of the Year.

When host Bob Hope presented Olga with the special Gilette Cavalcade award from America, she smiled shyly into the Russian TV cameras. "Thank you very much," she said, looking via satellite across the ocean. "My best wishes to my American friends."

"This proves one thing," comedian Hope replied, with nary a sign of a quip. "The world of sports can be a continuing key to improving international relations."

*Pig-tailed Russian gymnast Olga Korbut warmed the hearts of people all over the world when she won three gold medals and a silver at the 1972 Olympic Games in Munich, Germany.*

UPI

# HORSEBACK RIDING

## Pioneer on Horseback

### • ELEONORA SEARS

The Fifth Avenue strollers clutched their coats tightly about them in the chill of the January air. Suddenly the normal street noises of that day in 1912 were interrupted by the clatter of hoofbeats. Looking toward the street, startled pedestrians watched a coach with four galloping horses thunder down the avenue.

Seated high in the coachman's seat, expertly clutching the reins in white-gloved hands, was a thirty-one-year-old woman — head held boldly, eyes flashing with the pleasure and excitement of the ride. Miss Eleonora Sears, in response to a wager, was once again shocking American society by appearing in public in a traditionally male role — this time driving a four-in-hand like a professional coachman.

Eleo, the blonde, blue-eyed darling of Boston high society, was a great-great-grandaughter of Thomas Jefferson and the daughter of Frederick Sears, a wealthy shipping and real-estate tycoon. She was expected to conform to the conventions and proprieties of her time and position. Proper young ladies were seated in drawing rooms, sipping tea, not high in the seats of coaches behind galloping mares.

High-spirited Eleonora, born into se-

date society in 1881, was not content with a gentle game of croquet now and then. By the time she was in her teens she had begun her pilgrimage into the all-male world of sports, looking for excitement, competition, and perfection with the skill and persistence of any male athlete.

At night, elegantly gowned, she followed the social set from Boston to Newport, Rhode Island, from New York to Southampton, Long Island — dancing and frolicking with wealthy and titled young men until the wee hours of the morning. With the coming of daylight, she occupied herself with the forbidden pursuit of outdoor sports.

Eleonora's range of activities was incredible in those days, and even today. She was a whiz at tennis, drove a golf ball 200 yards, played polo like a cavalryman, and swam with the fishes. She would try anything on a dare and was among the first women to race a car and fly an airplane. She was the first of her sex to swim the 4½ miles from Bailey's Beach to First Beach along the elegant Newport shore. Even at such sports as hunting, fishing, and canoeing, she was an expert.

In 1910 a national magazine described

*A member of high Boston society in the early 1900s, liberated Eleonora Sears shocked the prudish American public by riding astride, racing cars, flying planes, and following such traditionally all-male pursuits as hunting, fishing, and canoeing.*

Miss Sears as "the best all-around athlete in American society." Yet, society did not praise Eleonora. It chastised her. When she appeared on an all-male polo field in 1912, wearing breeches instead of the traditional long skirt, and riding astride a pony instead of sidesaddle, she was censured. The Mothers' Club of Burlingame, California, angrily passed a public resolution denouncing her appearance:

> Such unconventional trousers and clothes of the masculine sex are contrary to the hard and fast customs of our ancestors. It is immodest and wholly unbecoming a woman, having a bad effect on the sensibilities of our boys and girls.

They demanded that Miss Sears "restrict herself to the usual feminine attire in the future." In other parts of the country, many sermons condemned her wickedness.

But Eleo, who had already been voted to society's "best-dressed list," was not to be restricted in her sporting costumes. Competition was the spice in her life and she continued to wear whatever she thought appropriate for comfort in sport. She adopted "shocking" outfits for swimming, sailing, figure skating, and tennis.

In her comfortable attire she became a champion at competitive tennis and squash. In tennis, she won the national doubles title four times and the mixed doubles once. She was a finalist in the singles twice. In squash, she was captain of the International Squash Racquets team, president of the Women's Squash Association, and the first national titleholder in 1928. In 1954, at seventy, she was still competing in the national squash championships.

When Eleo was in her forties, she took up her most attention-getting activity — long-distance walking. She made the headlines as a result of her annual 47-mile walk from Providence to Boston. Her fast-paced record for this stroll was 9 hours 53 minutes. She also walked 73 miles from Newport to Boston in 17 hours. Even when Eleo was in Europe, she went strolling. Once, when visiting France, she walked the 42½ miles from Fontainebleau to the Ritz Bar in Paris in 8½ hours.

Yet although Miss Sears' participated in many activities, her preoccupation with horses dominated her life. She was a superb horsewoman, riding in the steeplechase at horse shows and hunt meets. In later years, she devoted her time to raising championship horses for show as well as for racing. During most of her adult life she found time to ride at least four hours every day.

And as Eleonora Sears started out making news with horses, so she was to finish. In November 1967, the *New York Post* carried a feature story about Eleo:

. . . the regal, white-haired woman who sits in Box 72 [at the National Horse Show in Madison Square Garden] each night is Miss Eleonora Sears of Pride's Crossing, Massachusetts. She has had horses at the Garden every year since the National has been held. . . . This year she has two hunters in the show. Miss Sears has also loaned horses to the U.S. Equestrian team ever since it was founded. . . . Leafing back through 41 years of Garden programs, it is hard to find a show when a Sears horse didn't win blue ribbons. For many years, too, she rode them herself.

But Elenora would ride no more. She died in 1968 at the age of eighty-seven, gallant and energetic till the end.

# Two Crowns for the Princess

## • PRINCESS ANNE OF ENGLAND

Once upon a time there lived in England a beautiful young princess named Anne. From the time she was a very little girl, Anne loved horses and riding, and because she was a princess she could often ride the best steeds of her kingdom along the beautiful trails surrounding her home at Windsor Castle.

Anne was also encouraged to perfect her riding skills by her father, Prince Philip, who was the president of the International Equestrian Federation, and her mother, Queen Elizabeth, an expert horsewoman often seen astride a mount, reviewing her troops in her traditional role.

When the princess was seventeen years old, in 1968, she asked to be allowed to compete along with the commoners in her realm in the horse trials required for the Equestrian Championships of Europe. Her trainer, Allison Ower, found her to be an unusually able pupil, already well on the way to championship status.

In less than two years of hard riding and training the Princess qualified to compete in the grueling three-day European Equestrian Championships in the lush green countryside of Burghley, England.

When she appeared on her favorite horse, Doublet, on September 3, 1971, there was a record crowd of 20,000 adoring subjects cheering her on, including, of course, her mother the queen, and her father, Prince Philip.

Anne had previously been permitted to walk over the demanding cross-country course, but Doublet would have to depend on the sure hands of the princess to guide him while galloping at top speed over the unfamiliar ground. Although the princess had not been rated expert enough to be a member of the official British team, she scored in fast and faultless rounds over the steeplechase and cross-country sections of the course. When she entered the third and final day of competition, she held a comfortable lead.

The morning of September 5th shone bright and clear as the spunky princess once again mounted Doublet. The twenty-one-year-old rider gave her horse an affectionate pat of reassurance and they were off. Doublet did not let her down. In a flawless performance of jumping skills, he and the princess won the event, 37.8 points ahead of the other riders in the kingdom and the other eight nations competing. The championship was Anne's!

The princess received a motherly kiss from the queen and the coveted Raleigh Trophy from Prince Philip while her subjects shouted with pride and approval. She was the first royal rider ever to win the symbolic equestrian crown!

As the years went on the beautiful princess fell in love with and married a handsome commoner, Lieutenant Mark Phillips, who shared her love of riding, horses, and competition. Their future together was bright and they lived happily ever after, riding over the hills and dales of their British kingdom.

*Princess Anne of England acquired still another crown when she won the Raleigh Trophy at the European Equestrian Championships in 1971.*

UPI

# Leaping the Barrier

## • KATHY KUSNER

On October 22, 1968, Kathy Kusner, one of America's leading Olympic riders, was granted a jockey license by the Maryland Racing Commission. Until that time, women had not been permitted to ride on the thoroughbred race tracks of America. Kathy's historic victory for equality for her sex had been preceded, however, by a long list of her other victories as a horseback rider.

From the time Kathy joined the U.S. Olympic team in 1961, she had been a leading international dressage rider. The object of dressage is for the rider to show mastery over the horse through the use of very slight, but precise movements. Competitive dressage riding takes place in the show ring on specially trained horses. Kathy had competed in every recognized horse show in the world, winning most of the major prizes. She won the President's Cup in Washington, the New York championships in Madison Square Garden, the Prix des Amazones in Rotterdam, Holland, and the Irish Trophy in Dublin, Ireland, among others.

Kathy, who was born in 1940, was raised in the fox-hunting states of Virginia and Maryland. When she was ten, she had her own pony, which she kept in the backyard of her home in Arlington, Virginia. She cleaned out stables and groomed horses to earn board for her pony. Her father, a government mathematician, had little interest in horses, but he did believe his daughter should pursue whatever interested her.

Kathy was soon taking riding lessons and entering show and ring events. During her teens at Washington and Lee High School, she showed horses for dealers in Virginia and continued to ride, groom, and train whenever and wherever possible.

Her love for horses was all-consuming. "I want to ride forever," she said. She liked horses better than people and once commented to her father, "Wouldn't the world be a lot simpler if it were full of horses?"

When she was eighteen, Kathy set a women's horse-jump record (7 feet 3 inches), and in 1961 she became the first woman in ten years to join the U.S. equestrian team. She rode on the U.S. gold medal team in the Pan-American games in 1963 and again in the 1964

*Olympic equestrienne Kathy Kusner showed her championship style when she leaped a hurdle at the International Horse Show in New York in 1964.*

Olympics. In 1966, during a European tour, she won the International Grand Prix at Dublin as well as six other major European classes. She had taken the Dublin prize the year before and thus became the only rider in history to win this event twice in a row on the same horse — a spirited steed named Untouchable.

By 1967, Kathy had earned the reputation of leading equestrienne in the world. She was 103 pounds of champion in the only Olympic sport where men and women compete against each other. That year, the United States team consisted of seven members, four of whom were women. At the National Horse Show in Madison Square Garden, Kathy rode off with a major share of the honors, besting topflight riders from all over the world.

Yet, in spite of all Kathy's achievements, she still held on to what seemed to be an impossible dream. She wanted a jockey license.

In November, 1967, she applied to the Maryland Racing Commission for one. Although Judy Johnson had been granted a license in 1943 to ride in the steeplechase at the Pimlico (Maryland) track, no woman had yet been licensed to ride in the flat racing events. With the passage of a stronger Civil Rights Act in 1964, forbidding discrimination in employment because of sex, race, national origin, or religion, Kathy believed she had a good case. The Commission turned her down, but fortunately for the members of her sex, Kathy was not sidetracked from her purpose.

"Horse-riding is more a game of technique and skill than strength," she said. "It's the same as playing chess with men, so I don't intend to give up the fight."

After almost a year of court battles, Kathy's perseverance was rewarded. Judge Ernest A. Loveless overturned the Commission's ruling. "This court," stated the judge, "finds that no reasonable mind could possibly have reached the factual conclusion that the Maryland Commission did." The judge ordered a reversal on the grounds that Kathy's license had been refused on the basis of sex discrimination.

At the time of her scheduled debut on a Maryland track, Ms. Kusner was sidelined with a broken leg. But she did ride to victory in September, 1969, at Pocono Downs in Pennsylvania. While the determined Kathy Kusner accomplished her legal objective in securing a jockey's license, she was really an Olympian at heart. Still an amateur dressage rider, she competed with the cream of American riders in the 1968 and 1972 Olympics, winning a silver medal at Munich. She had come full circle.

# HORSE RACING

## The Lady Godivas and Their Handicaps

- **DIANE CRUMP**
- **PENNY ANN EARLY**
- **LINDA GOODWILL**
- **BARBARA JO RUBIN**
- **CHERYL WHITE**

Perhaps the most legendary equestrienne of all time was Lady Godiva, who, clothed only in her long golden tresses, rode bareback through the streets of Coventry, England, to protest the plight of the overtaxed poor more than nine hundred years ago.

On Sunday, April 20, 1969, a field of seven women jockeys on seven 3-year-old fillies raced down the track at Suffolk Downs in Boston in the first parimutuel horse race with an all female cast. They were competing for a $10,000 purse in the appropriately named Lady Godiva Stakes before a crowd of 18,940. What made the event most unusual and significant was that in 1969 in the state of Massachusetts there were seven fully licensed women jockeys. These jockeys — Penny Ann Early, Diane Crump, Tuesdee Testa, Brenda Wilson, Robyn Smith, Barbara Adler, and Connie Hendricks (in their finishing order) — had overcome a stableful of handicaps in order to achieve that title.

A little more than two years before the running of the Godiva Stakes, women jockeys were barred from riding on the parimutuel race tracks of the United States. Although Judy Johnson has been granted a license to ride in the steeplechase at Pimlico, Maryland, in 1943, no woman rider had yet come forward to demand equality with the men on the flat tracks. In a landmark decision Kathy Kusner became the first woman licensed to ride in thoroughbred horse races on October 22, 1968.

Following suit, the Kentucky Racing Commission granted a license to twenty-five-year-old Penny Ann Early. Unfortunately neither Penny or Kathy became the first woman jockey to ride against men. Penny encountered a boycott by male jockeys at Churchill Downs and Kathy was sidelined by a broken leg on the day of her scheduled debut.

The woman who did get to ride that premier race was Diane Crump, a shy, retiring 104-pound exercise groom, who rode her 50 to 1 shot, Bridle N' Bit, at Hialeah, Florida, on February 7, 1969. Although Diane finished tenth in this maiden gallop, she did become the first female to win a stakes race, at Spring Fiesta, New Orleans, a little over a month later. When the stalwart Ms. Crump mounted her three-year-old colt, Fathom, in Louisville, Kentucky, in the spring of 1970, she reached the goal sought by all jockeys — competition in the historic Kentucky Derby.

The starting gates were open, and the women were competing on all the major tracks in the country. Pert, pigtailed Barbara Jo Rubin made the scene first at Aqueduct, New York. At Charlestown, West Virginia, she became the first woman to win in a race against men, on February 22, 1969. She retired because of a torn cartilage in her knee but not before she had totaled eighty-nine rides — with twenty-two wins, ten seconds, and ten thirds.

Women jockeys came from all backgrounds, were young and older. Their common love was horses and racing. Names like Mary Bacon and Joan Phipps (they won the first daily double in New York); glamorous Robyn Smith, a former Hollywood movie starlet; Cheryl White, seventeen, black and beautiful from New Jersey; Tuesdee Testa, first to ride at Belmont Park, New York, were appearing on racing programs across the country. In England, Linda Goodwill received her professional jockey license from the British Jockey Club in 1975 to become Britain's first female jockey.

Indeed the handicaps had been overcome and the Lady Godivas of the world were donning their silks.

*Hard-riding Diane Crump was the first licensed female jockey to ride against men when she raced at Hialeah, Florida, in February, 1969.*

# Jockey With Nine Lives

## • MARY BACON

The young jockey accepted the award for the Philadelphia Sports Writers Association's Most Courageous Athlete of 1973. The denial in the acceptance speech carried through the dining room.

"I don't think I'm all that courageous," said the recipient. "I ride for the same reasons all jockeys do, to make a living. I ride because I love horses and not because I'm tough or brave."

But hardly any one of the 1,000 male diners at the awards dinner could believe these words. Mary Bacon, the twenty-three-year-old blonde pinup girl standing before them had just wound up another year of fierce riding in the dangerous, competitive business of thoroughbred racing, and everyone there knew how much courage that took for the female jockey.

Also, Mary held a track record for catastrophes. In 1969, after being thrown by a horse in Oklahoma, the 5 foot 4 inch jockey was hospitalized with a broken back. The resulting pinched spinal nerves left her paralyzed from the waist down for four days.

"I'll never forget lying there and trying so desperately to wiggle my toes," she re-called. "At times like that you think a lot about how short life is, and how you'd better make the most of your chances."

So back to the track she went with less than six weeks recovery time. One day after some hard riding in three consecutive races, she felt too ill to continue (two more races had been scheduled). After a quick call to her doctor, Mary admitted herself to the hospital, where her daughter Suzy was born several hours later. She had been riding while nine months pregnant!

In 1971, at Ellis Park in Owensburg, Kentucky, another fall from her horse resulted in a broken collarbone, leg contusions, bruised ribs, and internal bleeding. Yet thirteen days later, Mary rode again.

The following year she was thrown from her mount in a Pittsburgh race. This time another horse fell on top of her and everyone thought she had been killed. She remained unconscious for six days, and on the eleventh she left the hospital and headed straight for the track. She rode three races, winning one and placing third in another. "You can't quit because you've been thrown," said the still-hurting Ms. Bacon.

*Mary Bacon won the Philadelphia Sports Writers Association award for most Courageous Athlete of 1973.*

UPI

Being a woman racing against men made the going rougher for this beautiful young jockey. "From the moment that the starting gate opens until my horse hits the wire, I'm a man competing against men," she reasoned. But this shapely athlete who was a Playboy pinup for two years was no man by any standards. And she didn't have to put on an act to prove she was tough. All she had to do was win. And win she did. Once she and jockey Joan Phipps were the winners of the Daily Double at New York's Aqueduct race track — a first for women jockeys. It seemed a sure bet that no broken bones could break the spirit of the indomitable Mary Bacon.

# The Lady Was a Horse

## • RUFFIAN

Eighteen million people were watching the $350,000 match race on CBS-TV. A male was running against a female at Belmont Park, New York's most famous race track. It was the last day of the fourth-of-July weekend in 1975.

The lady's trainer, Frank Whiteley, Jr., never doubted for a moment that his racer was the fastest horse of her generation. She was far superior in appearance and natural ability to any other on the scene From the time she left the starting gate in her first race a little over a year earlier, Ruffian, as she was called, had never allowed a single competitor to get ahead of her. She had ten straight victories.

Her male rival, Foolish Pleasure, had won the Kentucky Derby, the most famous of all races. Still, Trainer LeRoy Jolley had worked ceaselessly to improve the speed of his sometimes erratic charge.

When final preparations were over, the three-year-old racers were led into the starting gate. They waited, with muscles tensed and rippling, for the signal. At last the moment arrived and the two bolted out onto the track.

Ruffian's time in the first quarter was a spectacular 22.2 seconds. The crowd was roaring with excitement as the sleek, dark-brown mare nosed ahead of her opponent.

Then came the break. Anyone close enough might have heard the sound — the crack of an ankle bone shattering. Ruffian's right leg collapsed under her. Still, the momentum of her tremendous speed kept her going forward and although she was in excruciating pain, she ran another 40 yards or so. That only further compounded the fracture and by the time the doctors rushed out to her, Ruffian had ground her ankle to a mass of splintered bone mixed with blood, sand, and grit.

Dr. Manuel Gilman, chief medico on New York race tracks for thirty-one years, was overwhelmed. "It was as bad an accident as could happen," he said. Even with four veterinarians and a skilled orthopedic surgeon working over her, the magnificent thoroughbred could not be saved.

Owner Stuart Janney made the final decision. . . . Ruffian was in too much pain, fright, and frenzy. She was too great a horse to have to suffer, and he gave the doctors the right to end her agony. "The best filly I'll ever see," he grieved.

The same thing that made her a winner, made her die. She ran too hard. It was her spirit that killed her. A broken-hearted stable hand may have provided the most fitting epitaph for this tragic champion. "She died in the lead," he said. "She will always be remembered as a winner."

*Filly Triple Crown winner Ruffian, ran with grace and style at the American Oaks race at Belmont Park in June, 1975. The jockey was Jacinto Vasquez.*

# SKIING

## America's First Golden Skier

### • GRETCHEN FRASER

Pert, pigtailed Gretchen Fraser waited tensely for the countdown to begin. In a few minutes she would be the first of thirty-one women skiers to rocket down the perilous Mt. Piz-Nair slope at the 1948 Winter Olympics in St. Moritz, Switzerland.

The phone at the starting gate rang, indicating that the slope was clear. "Five, four, three, two, one," counted the starter, and Gretchen poled off onto the treacherous course for the women's special slalom event.

Being first to go down the unblazed trail was a handicap, and Gretchen concentrated intently on the terrain ahead. She would have to weave in and out of the series of colorfully flagged poles, called gates, which were planted in the snow. She would have to execute clean, sharp turns while traveling at estimated speeds of close to 60 miles an hour. She would have to avoid hidden bumps in the snow, patches of ice, and other variations in the mountain's surface.

In less than a minute, Gretchen had reached the bottom. It was a flawless run, but because she had skied it first, she had lost precious seconds by using caution to track the course. The winner of this event, however, would be determined by the combined time of two runs, so Gretchen climbed back up the hill and readied herself once more at the starting gate.

This time she knew the slope and, literally throwing caution to the winds, zigzagged down without hesitation. In perfect control, she reached the bottom in 57.7 seconds. Her combined time, less than two minutes, gave her first place. A twenty-nine-year-old housewife had become America's first gold medalist in skiing. Since 1924, when the Winter Olympics were first held, Europeans had reigned supreme. Now an international unknown — and American as well — was queen of the slopes.

Although this was her first Olympic competition, Gretchen was not completely unknown to American skiers. Her mother, Norwegian by birth, was a ski enthusiast. After marrying William Kunigk of Tacoma, Washington, she worked for the development of Mt. Rainier as a public ski area and encouraged Americans to take up her favorite sport. Her name was familiar, and

*Gretchen Fraser was twenty-nine when she became America's first Olympic gold medalist in skiing at St. Moritz, Switzerland, in 1948.*

she was a popular figure on the northwestern ski slopes.

Although Gretchen started to ski competitively when she was only sixteen, it soon became her first love. To this she added her love for a fellow skier, Donald Fraser, a member of the 1936 Olympic ski team. By the time they were married, in 1939, Gretchen's skill on skis matched Donald's and the newlyweds both qualified for the 1940 Olympic team. World War II, however, caused the cancellation of the Games and Donald went off to serve four years in the Navy.

While he was away, Gretchen continued to build her own life. On the slopes, she became the first winner of the Diamond Sun event, held at Mt. Baldy in Sun Valley, Idaho. She won the same race the next year, 1941, and also the National Combined and Downhill championships.

In 1942, after becoming the National Slalom champion, Gretchen dropped out of competition to help in the war effort. She taught swimming, riding, and skiing to amputees in Army hospitals, and took flying lessons to fill her days. When Donald returned from the war, he encouraged his wife to resume her competitive skiing.

The day before Gretchen won her Olympic gold medal, the international crowd went wild when she won second place in the women's combined Alpine, a grueling test of speed and skill, which has since been discontinued as an Olympic event. After winning her gold medal, the unknown housewife from America shyly acknowledged the acclaim of fellow racers and spectators: "I had no idea I could do it," she said breathlessly. "My husband will be especially happy."

# On Olympian Slopes

## • ANDREA MEAD LAWRENCE

Andrea Mead was born in snowy New England in 1932, the year the Winter Olympics were held in the United States for the first time — at Lake Placid, New York. Andy's parents had established a ski area at Pico Peak, Vermont, and by the time the little girl was four, she was schussing down the hill in her own backyard.

Every year the family vacationed in Davos, Switzerland, not only to ski, but also to pick up tips for running their own ski area. In 1938, they brought back a well-known ski instructor, Carl Acker, to head the Pico Ski School. Andrea's lessons began in earnest.

By the time she was eleven, Andy was competing against adults. She took second in the Womens' Eastern Slalom Championship at Pico Peak in 1944. Two years later, while racing down the slope to help an injured skier, she broke her leg in the only ski accident of her career.

When she was fourteen, Andy qualified for the U.S. Olympic team at tryouts held at Sun Valley. In 1948 she went to St. Moritz, Switzerland, as the youngest member ever to be on a U.S. Olympic ski team. She finished eighth in the slalom, but she met young Dave Lawrence, a handsome teammate from Dartmouth College in New Hampshire.

Dave didn't give adolescent Andy a tumble until the 1949 tryouts for the FIS (*Federation Internationale de Ski*) team in Whitefish, Montana. Coming down the slope in a practice run, Dave lost control and tumbled at Andrea's feet. "She gave me a kind of scornful look, and it infuriated me," he said. So love bloomed.

The National Ski Association offered Andy and Dave a trip to Europe for pre-Olympic competition and practice. Andy won everything in sight, including Dave, and they were married in Davos before returning to Wyoming.

In 1952, Andy and Dave, who was chosen as an alternate on the men's team, left for the Winter games in Oslo. Andrea was an unusual competitior in at least one respect — she skied for fun and not necessarily to win. "I know it's the Olympics," she said. "Everybody wants to win, but honestly, I don't care. I just want to do my best."

Dave respected his wife's philosophy.

"I've learned never to wish her good luck on race day. It makes her mad. I just tell her to have fun."

On the day of the giant slalom, conditions were poor on the Norefjell course. The run was shortened to less than two thirds of a mile because of lack of snow. Some three hundred Norwegian soldiers had to shovel snow from the nearby gullies and ditches on to the bare spots on the mountain. Andrea was ready for the worst.

In a brilliant performance, however, she flew to victory before an audience that included such royalty as the princesses Ragnhild of Norway and Josephine-Charlotte of Belgium.

Three days later, in the special slalom race, Andy took a bad fall halfway down the hazardous Rodkleiva course. She finished the run, but it seemed unlikely that she could make up the valuable lost seconds her next time down. Determined to do her best anyway, Andrea shoved off with a hard, fast jump turn and continued the quick-poled turns through the 49 gates of the 508-yard course. On the last lap, she crouched daringly low and hugged the mountain the rest of the way down — literally into the waiting arms of her husband.

"Total time," blared the loudspeakers, "two minutes, ten and six-tenths seconds." Andrea had won another gold medal! This feat made her the only American skier, male or female, to achieve that distinction. If the male skiers couldn't reach Olympian heights, Andrea had proved a woman could.

*Andrea Mead Lawrence, who at fifteen was the youngest member of the Olympic ski team in 1948, won two gold medals at the 1952 Winter Games in Oslo, Norway.*     UPI

# The Family That Skis Together — Wins

- **BARBARA ANN COCHRAN**
- **LINDA COCHRAN**
- **MARILYN COCHRAN**

"See you at Cochran Hill in an hour," shouted the rosy-cheeked teen-ager to the group of friends standing outside Richmond High School. The snow was falling heavily and there was already an accumulation of several inches of new powder on the streets of this small northern Vermont community of 1200.

Cochran Hill was located just behind the old, rambling two-story farmhouse where Mickey and Virginia Cochran lived with their four children — Marilyn, Barbara Ann, Robert, and Linda. It was a gathering point for all the skiing youngsters in town. Mickey had been an international skier when he was younger, and this house in the heart of New England's ski country, with the homemade rope tow on the hill behind it, helped the Cochrans carry out their plan to make skiing a part of their family's way of life. But as every skier knows, it takes more than a heap of snow to make a champion skier, and this father had the know-how.

Mickey created a training program for his youngsters. It included a daily dose of push-ups, knee bends, cycling, weight lifting, and running. Although the children

grumbled, the workouts drew the family together and transformed the normal feelings of sibling rivalry into serious, but healthy, competitive sportsmanship.

It wasn't long before the Cochran children were outclassing all other skiers in their respective age-groups. Invariably they were their own major competition. In the early years, Marilyn, the eldest, usually beat the younger members of the family, including Bobby and his friends. When Barbara was thirteen in 1964 and she beat her older sister for the first time, the intensity of their rivalry increased. Even baby Linda, at eleven, began to show championship form. Whenever the girls skied together, there was always the inevitable question: which Cochran will win this time?

From 1968 to 1972 one Cochran or another could usually be found on the medal lists in this country's major meets. Marilyn, who was on a European tour in the winter of 1968–69, won a Giant Slalom in Austria and placed second in two World Cup events in Italy and Czechoslovakia.

Here in the United States, Barbara beat her sister in the U.S. National Giant

Linda Cochran, the youngest member of a fabulous skiing family, shows the skill that qualified her for the U.S. Olympic team in 1976.

Five-foot Barbara Cochran won America's first Olympic skiing medal in twenty years at Sapporo, Japan in 1972

Slalom championships in 1969 — her first major victory; and again in 1970, in the world championships, when she took second to her sister's third. The next year, however, Marilyn became the first American ever to win the French championships, while Barbara won the two World Cup events.

Marilyn, Barbara, and Bobby qualified for the fourteen-member U.S. Olympic ski team in Sapporo, Japan, in 1972. For the women's Special Slalom event, forty-two women would be competing in a race that would be won by the skier with the fastest combined time in two runs down the course. Marilyn, who fell early in her first run, turned her attention to cheering for her sister.

It was snowing fiercely by the time twenty-one-year-old Barbara was ready to start her second run. Her tiny, 5 foot ½ inch 120-pound frame hunched down low over her poles as she heard the starting gun. In a flurry of powder, she was off, snaking daringly through the 62 gates, hardly visible to the crowd lining the hill because of heavy fog and snow. When the electric scoreboard finally flashed her

combined time, the skiing Cochrans knew they had done it again. This time Barbara had won an Olympic gold medal — the first such victory for America since 1952!

Although that triumph was Barbara's, nobody could predict what the next run might bring. In 1975 twenty-one-year-old Linda took first place in the Giant Slalom, one of the European Cup events. She also had qualified for the Winter Olympics in Innsbruck, Austria. For a family as passionately devoted to skiing as the Cochrans, it seemed likely that a Cochran would win again — on one slope or another.

*The Skiing Cochrans, from left to right: Marilyn, Bobby, Barbara, father Mickey, and Linda.*

# Mother of the Hot Dog

## • SUZY CHAFFEE

Can you believe that tip rolls, outriggers, royals, worm turns, and 360's are just a few of the ingredients of the hot dog? Can't be, you say, but true it is. All those strange-sounding names are really maneuvers for a new, exciting, and creative American sport — freestyle skiing — more popularly known as "hot dogging."

A far cry from the traditional downhill or cross-country skills, which demand speed and endurance, hot dogging also includes any athletic stunt one can do in the air or on the slope, preferably without breaking a leg or tearing a muscle. The woman athlete who introduced all this to other women skiers was former Olympic downhiller Suzy Chaffee.

Suzy, born in 1947 in Rutland, Vermont, began skiing when she was three years old. By the time she was six, she was racing down the slopes around her New England hometown. At twenty, she had become America's number-one ranking female skier and the following year, 1968, she went to Grenoble, France, as captain of the U.S. Olympic ski team.

But Suzy was looking for greater thrills — beyond the slopes of alpine competition. She turned to the "hot dog," or freestyle, once a recreation for daredevil males only. When it became a professional sport in 1971, there was no separate division for women competitors, and Suzy skied head to head with the men. She was World Freestyle champion from 1971 to 1973. During those years, she encouraged more women to enter competition, and emphasized creativity, musical accompaniment, and the use of short skis.

In 1973, when the International Freestyle Association was formed, all of her ideas had become incorporated into the fabric of the sport. The women had their own contests and professionals like 1974 and 1975 world champion Genia Fuller, Marion Post, and Karen Huntoon were performing midair flips, airborne leaps, and balletlike groundwork with grace as well as agility and precision. The freestyle events that had evolved combined splashy showmanship with skill and courage. There was intense rivalry among the competitors who had to learn to ski spectacularly but with a constant eye on safety.

The events of the organized exhibitions and competitions included Stunt/Ballet,

Freestyle/Mogul, and Aerial/Acrobatic. The Stunt/Ballet was performed to music on a slight hill, using short skis to produce spins and gymnastic moves. In Freestyle/Mogul, the skier raced down a steep and challenging slope with treacherous terrain. The event was not judged for time but for the aggressive, creative way that the skier adapted his or her body to the natural contours of the mountain. The Aerial/Acrobatic part of the competition included maneuvers similar to those in springboard diving — mind-boggling gainers, kickouts, spread eagles, and flips.

Although freestyle skiing, an invention of American skiers had not yet become an Olympic event in 1976. Ms. Chaffee, who was on the board of directors of the U.S. Olympic Committee, looked forward to its acceptance one day as a bona fide amateur sport, fully sanctioned by the National Collegiate Athletic Association.

*Karen Huntoon, who placed third in the Colgate Women's Freestyle Championships in 1975, in one of the graceful ballet maneuvers incorporated into this new ski form.* COLGATE

*Daring and innovative Suzy Chaffee was America's first freestyle skiing champion, reigning from 1971-1973.* WIDE WORLD

# SOFTBALL
## The Fast Pitchers

- **JOAN JOYCE**
- **BERTHA REAGAN TICKEY**

When Joan Joyce was growing up in Waterbury, Connecticut, in the 1940s nobody objected to her love of sports. In fact, her parents and teachers, recognizing her natural talents, encouraged her. They never minded that she was a "tomboy."

Joan's mother was a factory worker, often getting home later than Mr. Joyce. Her father frequently took Joan and her brother to the local baseball park, where he coached several community teams. "Dad was a great player and in between times, we shagged flies or mimicked the pitchers and catchers," recalled Joan.

The summer of 1954, when she was not quite fourteen, Joan was invited to join the Brakettes, a women's softball team in Stratford, Connecticut, sponsored by the Raybestos Company. For the next three years Joan played organized ball, although she rarely pitched — only once, in fact.

At the final playoffs of the National Fast Pitch Softball Championships in 1957, she got her first big break. The Brakettes' star pitcher was Bertha Reagan Tickey, a forty-three-year-old grandmother, who would eventually wind up her career with a record of 735 victories, including 161

no-hitters. At the playoffs between the Brakettes and Fresno, Bertha hurt her arm, with the score 0-0. Joan was called in as a relief pitcher. Before 15,000 fans, she put on an amazing show and much to everyone's surprise pitched her first no-hitter, bringing the Brakettes the championship.

For the next seventeen years, as an amateur with the Brakettes, the 5 foot 9 inch Joan helped them pile up quite a record. With the winning of the 42nd Annual Fast Pitch Softball Tournament in 1973, the Connecticut ball players took their eleventh title (four in a row) and became the first team to hold the World and National Championships in the same year. Joan had pitched more than seventy no-hitters and achieved a batting average of more than .400. In January, 1974, she was given a gold key for outstanding achievement by the Sportswriters Association of Connecticut at their annual dinner. It was the first time in thirty-three years of presentations that the award went to a woman or a woman was invited to the dinner.

The cheerful blue-eyed brunette was a superb example of the all-around athlete of the '70s. Although she was a whiz on the mound, Joan was also a Connecticut bowling champion (only three months after taking up the sport), a superior golfer (13-handicap), and an outstanding basketball player (she once scored 54 points in one game).

During the summer of 1974, Joan joined the Brooklyn College faculty as instructor and coach of the softball and basketball teams. When she took on the softball varsity, they had already lost five out of the seven games they'd played. In two weeks, under her expert training, they began to win — eight games in a row. "That's why I love coaching," Joan said. "I can see the results vividly, sometimes immediately, and that's a great satisfaction."

On September 28, 1975, Joan Joyce left the amateur ranks to become a member of the newly formed International Women's Professional Softball Association. "Professional softball makes good family entertainment at a reasonable cost," she explained. And certainly women's softball is good entertainment. Joan proved it in an exhibition once when she struck out Hall of Fame baseball player Ted Williams.

*Most Valuable Player Joan Joyce (left) and Outstanding Pitcher Bertha Reagan Tickey accepted the championship trophy won by their team, the Brakettes, at the American Softball Association tournament in 1968.* WIDE WORLD

*Joan Joyce shows the winning form that brought the Brakettes the World Softball Championship in 1974, a first for an American team.* UPI

# SWIMMING

## Out of the Golden Age

- **ELEANOR HOLM**
- **HELENE MADISON**
- **KATHERINE RAWLS**

It took a long time for American bathers to finally become champion swimmers. And no wonder. In 1829, a writer surveying the women on the beaches, observed: "Some wear bloomers, buckled nattily about the waists . . . some are wrapped in crimson Turkish dressing gowns, and flounder through the water like long-legged flamingoes. Others are in pantaloons and worn-out jackets."

But the women finally shed their bloomers, thanks to such crusaders as Australia's Annette Kellerman; America's first Olympic freestyle gold medalist, Ethelda Bleibtrey; the first and youngest diving gold medalist, Aileen Riggin; and English Channel swimmer Gertrude Ederle. All through the 1920s, known as the Golden Age of Swimming, competitors from the Women's Swimming Association of New York were the leaders. Club members captured 132 national senior championships out of 193 competitions. In the 1920 Olympic Games at Antwerp, Belgium, American women won 4 of 5 events; in Paris in the 1924 Olympics they won 6 of 7; and in Amsterdam, Holland, in 1928, 5 of 7.

Perhaps the greatest swimmers to emerge from the golden age were Helene Madison, Katherine Rawls, and Eleanor Holm, all of whom were elected to the Helms Swimming Hall of Fame. In 1930, when Helene was seventeen, she held twenty-six world freestyle records in distances from 50 yards to 1 mile! The AAU said of her that no man or woman competitor under its aegis had ever equaled that feat. During the 1930s she captured twelve world and thirty American championships. She actually was the standard-holder of all the possible American freestyle events at one time.

During the Olympic Games in Los Angeles in 1932, Helene was America's only winner of three gold medals — the 100- and 400-meter freestyle and the 400-meter freestyle relay. The eighteen-year-old 6-footer from Seattle, Washington, was known as the queen of the waters. Also on the scene at that time, was Katherine Rawls, the only competitor on both the swimming and diving teams. She won a silver medal in springboard diving and, in the years to come, this versatile mermaid became champion in twenty-four swimming and five diving events.

Another teammate in the Los Angeles

*Helene Madison (left) won three gold medals in freestyle races and*
*Eleanor Holm one in the backstroke in the 1932 Olympics at Los Angeles.*

Olympics was beautiful Eleanor Holm, the gold medalist in the backstroke as well as a twelve-time national champion in that event. Besides her athletic accomplishments, the curvaceous Eleanor will be remembered as an entertainer — first as a singer in her first husband's (Art Jarrett) band, and then as the swim star of the famous New York World's Fair Aquacade, produced by her second husband, Billy Rose. In 1938, she went to Hollywood to play the role of Jane opposite Glenn Morris (the 1936 Olympic decathlon champion), who portrayed Tarzan of the Apes.

Although the "golden agers" of the past have been replaced by today's "water babies," their exploits are a part of the history and color of America's mermaids.

# The Biggest Splash

## •ANN CURTIS

The eleven-year-old swimmer took one last deep breath before churning to the end of the pool. As she slapped its side, young Ann Curtis of San Francisco knew she had just won her first major championship — the AAU girls freestyle. It would have been difficult to predict then that before her retirement from competition, this young swimmer would capture every American championship in the freestyle from 100 to 1500 meters. However, even this first victory made a surprising splash, since Ann had been taught to swim by the Sisters of the Ursuline Convent in Santa Rosa and not by a professional coach.

After this unexpected debut, Ann was invited to train with Charlie Sava, a famous West Coast coach who was noted for having turned out a bevy of champion swimmers from his Crystal Plunge pool. Under his tutelage, Ann had to swim an average of three miles a day — with no time off on Sundays. In less than two months the coach realized he had a very special fish in his pool, and began to include Ann in all his competitive meets.

Before she was seventeen, in 1943, Ann entered her first national championship in Shakamak Park, Indiana, where she won and set records in both the 400- and 880-yard freestyle, in addition to being high-point scorer. There then followed stellar performances in eleven consecutive meets in which she shattered numerous national marks. As a result of her spectacular achievements Ann was awarded the James E. Sullivan Memorial Trophy as the best amateur athlete of the year in 1944. The award had never gone to a woman or a swimmer before!

Her career was far from over. During the next five years she set four world freestyle records and eighteen American records, and she won thirty-one national championships. She was the first woman to swim 100 yards in less than 1 minute — 59.4 seconds. Her victories at the 1948 Olympics in London were recorded in the official record book: "Ann Curtis, United States aquatic great, took the 400-meter title, second in the 100, and also anchored the relay team to victory in a new Olympic record of 4:29.2 minutes.

Her relay stunt was hailed by many as the outstanding individual achievement of the entire Olympiad."

After her retirement from amateur competition in 1949, Ann married college basketball star Gordon Cuneo. She started her own swim club, where she devoted as many as fourteen hours a day to teaching children, including her own four, the techniques that had made her a champion.

*In 1944, Ann Curtis became the first woman—and the first swimmer—to win the James E. Sullivan Memorial Trophy as the year's most outstanding amateur athlete.* WIDE WORLD

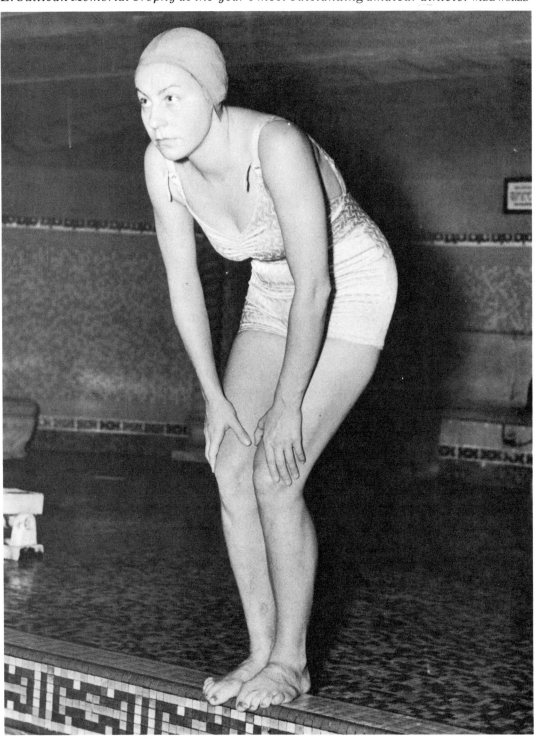

# The Inventive Aussies

• DAWN FRASER
• SHANE GOULD
• KAREN MORES
• JENNY TURRALL

There is no doubt that many records in sports don't last long. Someone always betters the athletic achievements of yesterday. But some marks last longer than others. Dawn Fraser, for example, was Australia's swim queen over a span of more than a dozen years, which is quite a feat in the annals of swimming.

Dawn was the gold medalist in the 100-meter freestyle for three Olympics — 1956, 1960, 1964. She held the world record in that event, 58.9 seconds, for almost the same length of time. In fact, the length of time the record lasted was a record in itself. Although America's age-group Water Babies came along to establish their marks in other world events, it took another swimmer from "down under" to equal and then better Dawn Fraser's time in the 100-meter freestyle.

Shane Gould was only fourteen and a half when she swam into history in that event. Even as an infant, Shane loved the water. She cried when bath time was over, and before she was three she could swim under water with her eyes open. Her family lived in the Fiji Islands until she was nine and during her days there she

learned to snorkel with a mask and fins and do a very respectable dog-paddle.

When the Goulds returned to the mainland to live in Sydney, Shane took her first lessons from a professional swim coach. In her competitive debut in the under-ten division of the New South Wales championships, she won a silver medal in the

*Fifteen-year-old Australian Shane Gould holds up her country's mascot after winning three gold medals in the 1972 Olympics in Munich, Germany.* UPI

breaststroke. But her entrance into the record books came five years later, in 1971.

During that year, Shane equaled or bettered seven record clockings, starting in April, when she matched Dawn Fraser in the 100-meter freestyle. In May she swam the 200-meters in .2 seconds less than American Debbie Meyer; in July she took the 400-meter record from teammate Karen Mores; in November she broke her own 200-meter mark; and in December she cracked both the 800- and 1500-meter standards.

Shane was typical of the youthful swim stars of the period. She spent long hours practicing while trying to keep up the normal life of a teen-ager. With braces on her teeth and a teddy bear still on her pillow, this youngster won two individual freestyle gold medals in the 1972 Olympic Games at Munich, Germany. She also was victorious in the 200-meter medley.

By 1975, however, Shane's records went the way of all records. Kornelia Ender of East Germany had shaved off two seconds from the 100-meter freestyle; Shirley Babashoff of the United States set new marks in the 200- and 400-meters; and a fellow Australian, Jenny Turrall, posted record clockings at 800 and 1500 meters.

But no matter. It seems likely that there will always be an Australian swimmer listed among current record holders. After all, the "Australian crawl" is credited as the forerunner of today's freestyle — and Annette Kellerman is credited with having brought the first freestyle bathing suit to the world's "bloomered" swimmers.

*Jenny Turrall, who was only thirteen at the time set a world record in the 1500-meter freestyle at Sydney, Australia, in 1973.* UPI

*Australia's swim champion Annette Kellerman was arrested for indecent exposure when she appeared in 1907 on a Boston beach, wearing a one-piece stretch suit like this.*
WIDE WORLD

# The Water Babies

- **SHIRLEY BABASHOFF**
- **MELISSA BELOTE**
- **DEBBIE MEYER**
- **CHRIS von SALTZA**
- **SHARON STOUDER**

During the 1950s, Australian swimmers dominated the water world. With the exception of Shelley Mann, who won the 100-meter butterfly in the 1956 Olympics at Melbourne, Australia, and was America's first four-stroke medley champion, there were no bright stars among the United States women. The country needed fresh, new swimming talent, and so a nationwide program was launched. Under the direction of George Haines, head coach of the Santa Clara (California) Swim Club, Beth Kaufman, and Dr. Sammy Lee, two-time Olympic gold medalist in diving, the Amateur Athletic Union embarked on its age-group development program.

Concentrating on boys and girls from eight to seventeen, local swim clubs were set up all over the country, with emphasis on good coaching and frequent competition. It was hoped that early training would bring up the level of United States competitors.

In 1956, a perky twelve-year-old was a member of Haines's Santa Clara team. The pre-teen Chris von Saltza had narrowly missed making the Olympic squad that year, and determinedly set her sights on the 1960 Games. During the next four years she was a fairly consistent winner in local and national meets, breaking many of her age-group records.

Chris had the ability to get the most out of her day, and although swimming practice dominated most of her time, she also managed to lead a normal teen-ager's life. Besides being a straight-A student at Los Gatos High School, a member of the student council, and secretary of her class, Chris was also a cheerleader and had to attend most of the high school sports events. Most important, she swam well enough to reach her goal — the Rome Olympic Games.

As a result of the age-group program, the women's squad in 1960 included fourteen swimmers and three divers whose ages averaged only sixteen-and-a-half years. Thirteen-year-old Donna deVarona was the youngest member, and Sylvia Ruuska, two-time Olympian, the oldest at eighteen.

The Water Babies, as they were called, made a spectacular splash — with sweet-sixteen-year-old Chris leading the way.

*Four of the Water Babies (left to right), Lynn Burke, Chris von Saltza, Patty Kempner, and Carolyn Schuler, after winning their gold medals in the 400-meter relay at the Rome Olympic Games.*                                                    UPI

She won three gold medals and a silver. The firsts were in the 400-meter freestyle and the 400-meter medley and freestyle relays. Dawn Fraser, the reigning Australian queen, defeated Chris in the 100-meter freestyle, but only by six-tenths of a second. Ms. Fraser's gold was the only victory for the Australian women swimmers in this Olympics.

Chris's golden teammates were Joan Spillane, Shirley Stobs, and Carolyn Wood in the medley, and Lynn Burke, Patty Kempner, and Carolyn Schuler in the freestyle. Lynn Burke also won another gold medal in the 100-meter backstroke; and Carolyn Schuler was the winner in the butterfly.

Even off the board the United States youngsters made a good showing. Paula Jean Pope of Santa Ana, California, took home two silver medals in springboard and platform diving. Altogether the amazing Water Babies were victorious in five out of the nine water events and came

in second in three. Before the Games were over they had set three world records as well.

The Australians' streak had been broken and the Americans were in the swim again. They showed it in the 1964 Olympics, when they were victorious in seven out of ten events. The leader this time was fifteen-year-old Sharon Stouder from Glendora, California. Like Chris, Sharon won three gold medals and a silver — setting a world record in the 100-meter butterfly. Although Sharon lost to Dawn Fraser in the 100-meter freestyle by only a stroke, she was the first American girl to break one minute in that event. Donna deVarona, now seventeen, took two gold medals home, and teammates Cynthia Goyette, Sharon Finneran, Martha Randall, Lillian Watson, Kathleen Ellis, Virginia Duenkel, and Cathy Ferguson took one apiece. Leslie Bush was the gold medalist in the platform dive.

In 1968 another teen-ager left her mark

on the swimming world. Debbie Meyer, sixteen, a short-haired brunette from Sherman Chavoor's Arden Hills Swim Club in Sacramento, California, held world records in the 400-, 800-, and 1500-meter, as well as the 880-yard event. Bob Paul, a U.S. Olympic committee official, said she had the most beautiful freestyle stroke he had ever seen.

Debbie had been named by *Tass*, the official Soviet News agency, as Sportswoman of the Year 1967, following a poll of thirteen news bureaus in Europe, the United States, and Asia. Two other young swimmers were named in the poll — Claudia Kolb, world record-holder at 200 and 400 meters, and Catie Ball, world breaststroke champion. These youngsters, along with Kaye Hall, Jan Henne, Lillian Watson, Sharon Wichman, Jane Barkman, Linda Gustavson, Sue Pederson, Ellie Daniel, and Sue Gossick (diving) were victorious in twelve out of sixteen individual or relay events at the Olympic Games in Mexico City.

Debbie became the first swimmer in history to capture three individual gold medals in a single Olympics. Before the year was over, in addition to holding four world records, she had become the fourth female winner of the Sullivan Award as America's outstanding amateur athlete.

The list of American medal winners and world-record breakers continues to grow — always new names, always young. With Melissa Belote at the top in three first places, the 1972 Olympics also brought gold medals to Sandra Neilson, Keena Rothhammer, Cathy Carr, Deena Deardruff, Jennifer Kemp, Jane Barkman, Shirley Babashoff, Karen Moe, and Micki King (diving). Looking ahead to the Games in 1976, Shirley Babashoff and Kathy Heddy seemed likely to make the biggest splash.

The water babies of America will come and go. Youngsters like Chris von Saltza, who went on to college and then to the Peace Corps, will find other pleasures and satisfactions in life. But for one brief moment, while still in their teens, they are the glittering stars in Olympic waters. America seems destined to continue giving birth to new water babies.

*Melissa Belote, America's top back-stroker at the Munich Games in 1972, set the world record for the 200-meter backstroke in addition to winning two other gold medals.*　　UPI

*Shirley Babashoff, the 1975 world champion in the 200-and 400-meter freestyle, came in second in the 100-meter and third in the 800-meter.*　　UPI

# Across the Channel and Back

• **FLORENCE CHADWICK**
• **GERTRUDE EDERLE**

The tugboat *Macom* moved slowly into New York Harbor. Every steamship within range had tied down its whistle cord in open position, sirens from small craft close by blasted forth in one continuous wail, and airplanes swooped low in salute while dropping flowers on the deck of the tug.

Standing at the bow, surrounded by masses of crushed petals, reporters and city dignitaries in frock coats and striped trousers was an apple-cheeked, cherubic-looking girl of nineteen. She reached out as if to embrace the noise. For this giant salute was for her, Gertrude "Trudy" Ederle, daughter of a New York City butcher, who on August 6th, 1926, became the first woman to swim the 20 miles across the English Channel. Furthermore, she'd done so in the record-breaking time of 14 hours and 31 minutes.

Until that day in August, only five men had succeeded in conquering the Channel, and the record had stood at a little over 16½ hours. Now the world had a new record-holder, and it was a 5 foot 5 inch woman.

Trudy was a humble girl with a whole-some and happy disposition. When she was thirteen she had joined the Women's Swimming Association, a swim club on the lower east side of Manhattan. For a city child usually surrounded by soot and cement, it was a real joy to escape to the cool refreshing waters of the pool. Her joy soon became a passion and in less than a year, she began to spend most of her time in the water. In the international 3-mile swim for J.P. Day Cup in 1921, she earned her first record. Swimming in that New York Bay race, she defeated more than fifty of the world's outstanding swimmers. And this was the first time she had ever competed in a race of over 220 yards.

By 1924, when she was only seventeen, Trudy held eighteen world's distance records. At the Olympic Games in Paris that year, she won a gold medal as member of the U.S. 400-meter relay team and two bronze medals for placing third in the 100- and 400-meter freestyle races.

A month after she became the first woman to swim the English Channel, an editorial appeared in the *Saturday Evening Post*. "Her (Gertrude Ederle) youth and gay courage captured the imagination of all continents. . . . In all the annals of sport there is no finer record than that hung up by this young American girl. . . . There is every reason to hope and believe that Miss Ederle's great achievement will intensify interest in distance swimming as a sport for both men and women."

And it did. In fact, the same year Trudy made her record-breaking swim, a child of ten was making her first marathon attempt across the channel at the mouth of San Diego Bay in California.

The youngster, Florence Chadwick, daughter of a detective with the San Diego Police Department, showed early signs of becoming a champion. Winning her first race in a local pool when she was only six, she went on to become winner of the annual 2½ mile race at La Jolla, California, ten times.

But Florence's goals were to encompass wider waters. By 1950, swimming the Channel from France to England had become a fairly common achievement. Florence had done it in June of that year. Now she started training to swim back in the other direction, from England to France, against the tides and winds. It was a swim considered virtually impossible, even foolhardy.

*Gertrude Ederle enters the water at Cape Gris-Nez, France, on the way to becoming the first woman to swim the English Channel in 1926.* UPI

*In 1951 Florence Chadwick became the only woman ever to swim the English Channel from England to France as well as from France to England.* WIDE WORLD

For eleven weeks Ms. Chadwick waited in a Dover, England, hotel for weather and sea conditions to be right for the attempt. She gorged herself with starches and ice cream to put extra fat on her body. She averaged about three or four hours daily in the water and was in bed by nine-thirty every night in the hope that the next day would be acceptable for her attack on the Channel. But the poor conditions did not improve.

Finally, on an August morning in a soupy fog, against unfavorable tide, and in waves heavily tipped with whitecaps, Florence got tired of waiting and took the plunge.

The water was icy cold. In less than three hours, she was overcome by severe nausea, and her trainer had to give her sea-sickness pills. The queasiness soon passed but now she had another, more formidable, foe — the terrible cold. The coat of protective grease on her body had washed off and her arms and legs were numb. The fog was so thick she couldn't even see the boat cruising alongside. Every stroke was an agony and she had slowed down almost to treading water.

At last, 16 hours and 22 minutes after starting out, Florence dragged herself ashore. With her hands and body cut and bruised by offshore rocks, she shook hands with the Mayor of Sangatte, France.

Florence Chadwick had achieved her goal. At thirty-three years of age, she had become the first woman in the world to swim the English Channel in both directions!

# In the Jaws of the Deep

### • LYNNE COX
### • DIANA NYAD

There is an old fable told by the Maori tribesmen of New Zealand about a husband and wife who lived on South Island many moons ago. The husband, who had fallen in love with a younger woman, decided to get rid of his spouse. He paddled her across the 13½ miles of the treacherous waters of Cook Strait to North Island and left her ashore to die, while he returned to the arms of his waiting lover. The wife, in desperation and anger, prayed to the gods for salvation and revenge. Her prayers were answered and with the aid of a god-sent dolphin, she swam back across the Strait to the safety of her home, whereupon a sudden storm wiped out all traces of her faithless husband and his lover.

A story told in 1975 was no fable. The gods had nothing to do with the miraculous marathon swim of eighteen-year-old Lynne Cox, who was the first woman to swim across Cook Strait. For 12 hours and 3 minutes, with no dolphin to guide her, Lynne battled the 25-knot winds and 5-foot swells from Ohau Point, North Island, to the kelp-covered rocks off South Island. The fierce and unpredictable tides and currents made it one of the most difficult of all long-distance swims. The Strait was conquered thirty-four years after the first attempt to cross it — and then there were only two successes in twenty tries.

When she was only thirteen, the teenager who accomplished this feat had already spanned the 21-mile stretch of California's Catalina Channel and then turned her sights on the Mt. Everest of marathon swims — the English Channel.

In 1972, of the 1,400 swimmers who had attempted the Channel crossing since 1875, only 200 had made it, 40 of them women. The memory of the first of these, Gertrude Ederle, who had battled the icy waters for 14 hours and 31 minutes in 1926, was firmly etched in Lynne's mind. The young swimmer also wanted to make history, and on July 20 she did, setting the record by swimming from England to France in 9 hours and 57 minutes.

But as all records have a way of being broken, an Army lieutenant, Richard David, spanned the Channel in 13 minutes less time. Fifteen-year-old Lynne would not let this faze her. The following year she returned to Dover, where she once again set the record. This time, the all-time male or female clocking was 9 hours and 36 minutes!

It is not unusual for marathon swimmers to make more than one attempt in a given body of water, since conditions such as water and air temperatures, winds and tides can play havoc with even the best-prepared athletes. In fall, 1975, Diana Nyad, a twenty-five-year-old New Yorker, set out to swim around Manhattan Island. Her try was aborted by severe cold and almost constant wind and rain. And then, as if defeat were not enough, the exhausted swimmer came down with a severe virus, presumably caused by the polluted waters of the Hudson River.

Eleven days later, on October 5, the well-greased Ms. Nyad (naiad means water nymph in Greek), was back in the Hudson again, this time under highly favorable conditions. She was ahead of her own schedule from the start, passing through Hell Gate, the most treacherous part of the trip, ten minutes before high tide. Exhausted but victorious, Diana was pulled out of the filthy waters of the East River, just north of Gracie Mansion, the mayor's residence. It had taken her 7 hours and 57 minutes, breaking the old record that had been set by Byron Somers almost half a century before!

Although neither of these extraordinary long-distance swimmers, Diana or Lynne, had ever encountered the jaws of a shark, the trials they had overcome often seemed equally formidable. In 1974, when Lynne was swimming in the hot, muddy waters of the River Nile, she had passed such creatures as dead dogs and live alligators. Determined marathoners like Diana and Lynne don't let anything get in the way.

*Marathon swimmer Diana Nyad made the journey around Manhattan Island on October 5, 1975.* WIDE WORLD

*Eighteen-year-old Lynne Cox prepares to conquer Cook Strait, the treacherous 14-mile stretch between the North and South islands of New Zealand, on February 4, 1975.* WIDE WORLD

# DIVING

## On Top of the High Board

### • PATRICIA McCORMICK

Poised 33 feet above the water on the high platform, she looked more like an aerial acrobat in trim circus tights than a diver. Running through her carefully placed three steps to the edge of the platform, twenty-one-year-old Pat Keller McCormick bounded into the air before twisting her lithe body into a spectacular dive.

Momentarily the 5 foot 4 inch, 125-pound athlete was hanging in the face-upward, horizontal position of the half gainer, with her head toward the board. At the peak of her lift, she rolled over in a half-twist that put her in a swan position. Now on her stomach, she went into her tuck, grabbing her legs above the ankles and hugging her knees close to her breast, before revolving in a complete somersault. After another half somersault, she cleanly pierced the water at the Los Angeles Stadium pool.

While performing these acrobatics, Pat was clocked through the air at the rate of 68 miles per hour. Her dive, executed with such ease and precision, was rarely attempted by men and was no longer permitted in women's Olympic competition because of its obvious hazards. Pat was

doing this dive for practice because she was training for the 1952 Olympics.

With two long strokes, she reached the side of the pool, pulled herself up and over the edge, grabbed her towel, and hurried to the locker room. This September day in 1951 had been a particularly exhausting one. At nine in the morning she had arrived at the pool for a 2½ hour drill on the high tower. At one o'clock, after lunch and a short nap, she had practiced her springboard dives. From two-thirty to four she was home, doing her housework, shopping, and preparing dinner for her husband, Glenn. Now it was nearly seven-thirty, and Pat had finally completed her last 3 hour session.

Wearily, she pulled the wool sweater over her head. She was so tired that she decided to see the club doctor the next day to make sure she was in good enough condition to continue her training — eleven more months, 80 to 100 dives a day, six days a week, 2,200 climbs up the diving board ladder every month.

After a thorough physical examination, Pat was relieved to find nothing seriously wrong. However, the doctor noted on his

*Sullivan Award winner Patricia McCormick was the only diver ever to win two gold medals in consecutive Olympic Games—1952 and 1956.*                    WIDE WORLD

chart that Mrs. McCormick had a 6-inch healed-over scalp wound, several prominent scars at the base of her spine, fresh lacerations of the feet and elbows, a once-cracked rib and broken finger, a loose jaw that threatened to pop from its hinges, and a number of ugly welts across her collarbones.

"I've seen worse casualty cases," he told Pat, "but only where a building caved in." These were all diving injuries of the past. What Pat needed now was some rest and a supplementary dose of vitamins.

What kind of woman subjected herself daily to the dangers of a sport like high diving? Pat McCormick was a United States champion. In 1950, she had become the first woman to sweep all three National Amateur Athletic Union outdoor diving crowns. In 1951, she also won all the AAU indoor titles.

As a toddler, Pat rode the breakers at Seal Beach near Santa Monica, California.

She grew up unafraid of the water. In her teens she spent all her spare time at Long Beach Lagoon and Muscle Beach, where she quickly developed into an aerial acrobat, tossed in and out of the surf by the strong, young crowd of exuberant surfers. At fourteen she won her first diving trophy, the Long Beach One-Meter Gold Cup.

In 1952, after six years of strenuous, often dangerous, competition, Pat was ready to make her Olympic debut in Helsinki, Finland. She proved to be the greatest diving queen the world had ever known. That year she won both diving events — springboard and platform — and four years later repeated her gold-medal performance in the Olympics at Melbourne, Australia. Her record has never been duplicated. For her achievements, Pat was awarded the Sullivan Memorial Trophy in 1956 as the nation's number-one amateur athlete.

# Flying High

## • CAPTAIN MAXINE "MICKI" KING

Aileen Riggin, America's first and youngest Olympic gold medalist in diving, was only thirteen years old when she won the springboard event at Antwerp, Belgium, in 1920. In the years that followed, such other Americans as Georgia Coleman, Dorothy Poynton-Hill, Victoria Draves, Marjorie Gestring (also thirteen), Pat McCormick, Leslie Bush, and Sue Gossick continued this country's domination of the international and national diving competitions.

Yet, in spite of all these successes, no victory seemed quite as sweet as that of Captain Micki King of the U.S. Air Force, who reached her pinnacle in Munich in 1972, when she was twenty-seven years old.

When Micki was a youngster growing up in Pontiac, Michigan, she loved water sports. Although she started diving when she was ten, it was only for fun and when she went off to college in 1962, Micki's varsity sport was the wet and warring game of water polo. Her coach at the University of Michigan, Dick Kimball, considered her one of the best female water-polo players in the country. She was

a star goalie and made All-American in 1962 and 1963. Yet he also saw in her a raw talent for diving, and encouraged her to start taking it seriously.

From 1963 to 1966 Micki was the sensation of the Big Ten diving teams, but with graduation close at hand, she would soon have to give up competition altogether and get a job. She couldn't ask her family to support her while she continued a career in amateur athletics.

The solution to her dilemma came from an unexpected source — the United States Air Force. Micki enlisted in the Corps as an officer candidate and in the fall of 1966 received her commission as a 2nd lieutenant. She was assigned to work at the University of Michigan with the Reserve Officer Training Corps. There she was able to continue her diving under Coach Kimball, while carrying out her duties for the Air Force.

It was a strenuous schedule, but her efforts paid off. By the time the 1968 Olympics rolled around, Micki easily qualified for the team. Most observers felt she'd win a gold medal in Mexico City. Her almost perfect form in the required dives, along with her unequaled performance in the optional ones, brought her to the finals as expected.

On her next to the last dive, with victory almost certain, Micki sprung off the board for a reverse 1½ layout. Too much height she sensed — and she quickly tried to adjust by throwing out her arms on the movement downward. As she passed the board, her forearm cracked into the wood, and in that sickening moment she knew all was lost. Although she felt excruciating pain and thought her arm might be broken, she returned to the high board and finished the competition — only to come in fourth.

It was a bitter defeat and Micki, after returning home, was transferred to the Los Angeles Air Force Station. She believed she was finished with diving for good. Once again the Air Force rescued her when they suggested she represent them in the World Military Games in Pes-

cora, Italy. Micki, the only woman in the competition, won a bronze medal.

Convinced that she still had some good diving years left, Micki continued to compete in the AAU championships and the Pan-American Games. After she was promoted to captain she became the only woman in the athletic department at the Air Force Academy in Colorado. Mother Max, as the cadets called her, qualified for the U.S. Olympic team to compete in Munich in 1972. She was in excellent physical shape and at the peak of her diving form. This time she dived to victory in the springboard event with almost flawless precision.

Captain King wept quietly when they hung the gold medal around her neck. "I've been diving longer than the girl who came in second has lived," she said later. Sky King, after eighteen years on the high board, had finally reached her full height as a diver.

*Captain Micki King, winner of the Olympic gold medal in springboard diving at Munich in 1972, became the only woman instructor in the athletic department at the U.S. Air Force Academy in Colorado.* UPI

# TENNIS

## In the Grand Tradition

### •HAZEL HOTCHKISS WIGHTMAN

A dozen years after Mary Ewing Outerbridge brought the game of tennis to America from Bermuda in 1874, a delicate, ailing little girl was born in Healdsburg, California. Until she was fourteen, Hazel Hotchkiss lived on a 1,500 acre ranch in a remote unpopulated area. There wasn't much to do but enjoy the outdoors and Hazel's four brothers were instructed to include her in all their games. It was the doctor's prescription for her poor health, and it worked. She grew stronger and stronger, playing all sorts of sports. By the time the family moved to Berkeley, she was considered too old to play with the boys, and her parents set up a gravel area in front of the garage to teach her the more "genteel" game of tennis.

In 1902, six months after taking up a racket, Hazel entered her first tournament and won. Playing with Mary Radcliffe in the Bay County Women's Doubles Championships, she introduced the volley and net play into the game. Women's place had always been at the base line, and these new tactics began the emancipation of women's tennis.

In those early days, at the turn of the century, five Sutton sisters led by May and Florence dominated California tennis. A popular slogan, "It takes a Sutton to beat a Sutton," was finally changed to, "It takes a Hotchkiss to beat a Sutton," as Hazel competed across the state. In 1909 Hazel went East, where she won her first national grand slam — singles, doubles, and mixed doubles — a feat she repeated in 1910 and 1911. During a spectacular span of nearly sixty years, Hazel won about sixty championships in the United States. Her last winning tournament was played in 1954, when she took the national senior doubles title. And she was still playing doubles in her mid-seventies in 1961.

As the wife of George Wightman, a past president of the U.S. Lawn Tennis Association, Ms. Wightman raised five children. In 1923 she donated a silver trophy to the USLTA "for competition among women's teams throughout the world." Only England and the United States have competed through the years, with Great Britain taking the cup seven times during a half-century of competitions. Ms. Wightman herself was a playing or nonplaying captain of the U.S. team thirteen times.

*Hazel Hotchkiss Wightman, one of America's earliest tennis champions and donor of the Wightman Cup, was playing and teaching the game well into her eighties.*  UPI

The ageless Ms. Wightman never really "retired" from tennis. Until her death at the age of eighty-seven, in 1974, she actively taught the game and played hostess to the new crop of young tennis stars at her large rambling home in Chestnut Hill, Massachusetts. At the height of her career Ms. Wightman wrote a book called *Better Tennis*. Included in her homespun advice was an alphabet of alliterative maxims starting with ALWAYS ALERT, BE BETTER, CONCENTRATE CONSTANTLY, and ending with QUASH QUALMS, UMPIRE USUALLY, XCEED EXPECTATIONS, and ZIP ZIP. Hazel Hotchkiss Wightman was one tennis player who never lost her ZIP ZIP!

Revered as the queen mother of American tennis, this grande dame was made a commander of the British Empire when she was eighty-seven years old. The award was presented to her by the queen mother of England herself.

# Gift From Norway

## • MOLLA BJURSTEDT MALLORY
## • HELEN HULL JACOBS

When Molla Bjurstedt came to America in 1915, she was already known as the first lady of Norwegian tennis. In her initial bid for the U.S. national championship that year, the twenty-three-year-old Norwegian defeated Hazel Wightman in a match in which a writer described Molla as "a panther stalking her prey."

That aggressive style revolutionized women's tennis in America by forcing competitors into a hard-hitting baseline game. Molla was always on the attack, playing with driving, smashing force. Over a period of a dozen years, she won eight national titles until 1926, a record number that has never been equaled.

The highlight of Molla's career came in 1921 at the Nationals in Forest Hills, New York, when she faced the undefeated French champion, Suzanne Lenglen, in the first round. It was one of the most dramatic matches of all time, with Molla winning the first set, 6–2. Mademoiselle Lenglen, after losing the first point at the opening of the second set, suddenly stopped the game and walked off the court in default. Molla had played spectacular tennis, and there seemed little doubt as to

who would have won had the match continued. Molla was the only competitor to defeat the incomparable Suzanne Lenglen from the time the French woman first won at Wimbledon in 1919 until she turned pro in 1926.

Molla had married a stockbroker, Franklin Mallory, and after his death in 1934, was forced to leave the life of wealth

*A 1918 look at tennis stars Molla Mallory (left) and all-around athlete Eleonora Sears, who teamed to win the National Women's Doubles Championship in 1916 and 1917.* UPI

and social prestige she had long enjoyed. She went to work in government service, keeping only one small trophy from the hundreds she had won in her days of glory. Her courage and adaptability may have been the qualities that made her the winner she was.

In 1944, four-time national tennis champion, Helen Hull Jacobs, wrote a book about the greats of the game. *Gallery of Champions* included such women stars as Alice Marble, Pauline Betz, and Louise Brough along with Suzanne Lenglen and Molla. The dedication read: "To Molla Mallory, whose domination of American women's tennis was less important than the legacy she left to those who came after her. Her great driving game was the beginning of an era of hard-hitters among women players. I think that her courage and sportsmanship and, above all, her will to win were a contribution of unforgettable value."

What a special person Molla Bjurstedt Mallory must have been to have inspired such a tribute from a fellow competitor. She was most certainly Norway's gift to American tennis.

*Helen Hull Jacobs, tennis star and author, at Forest Hills, where she won the National Championship in 1936.*
UPI

# Madamoiselle De La Court

## • SUZANNE LENGLEN

On the night of October 9, 1926, Madamoiselle Suzanne Lenglen, France's court ballerina, toast of Paris, and queen of Wimbledon, made her professional tennis debut at Madison Square Garden in New York City before a sophisticated audience of 13,000. It was a historic event for the American tennis world because it marked the start of the professional tennis tour in this country and included a cast of such champions as Vincent Richards, Bill Johnston, and Mary Browne.

However, it was largely the presence of the incomparable Suzanne that accounted for the packed arena. Her reputation had been carried across the ocean for many years, and she did not disappoint the curious spectators. In the manner of a cool, assured master of the courts, Mlle. Lenglen made short work of Mary Browne, 6–1, 6–1.

Suzanne had been a sickly child. She was coached by her father, Charles, who was the secretary of a tennis club in Nice, France. "Papa" set out to make his frail daughter a strong, outstanding athlete. Although she continued to suffer from ill health, Suzanne did become a great tennis player. She competed in her first tournament when she was twelve, astonishing everyone with her command of the game and her graceful, yet powerful, technique. She became France's singles and doubles hard-court champion when she was fifteen in 1914.

Mlle. Lenglen took the first of her six victories at Wimbledon in 1919, when she defeated six-time British winner Mrs. Dorothy Douglass Chambers. That match is still considered to be one of the most thrilling of all time. Twenty-year-old Suzanne was victorious after forty-four grueling games — 10–8, 4–6, 9–7.

Watching Suzanne play was a joy for her fans here and abroad. She could leap in the air with the ease of a dancer, often pirouetting after a ball that seemed likely to elude her. "I just throw dignity to the winds and think of nothing but the game," she said when asked about her unorthodox style. But unorthodox or not, everyone tried to copy not only her ballerinalike movements but also her clothes and manner of walking and talking. Her legion of followers put her in the category of a demigod.

The "maid marvel" continued to flash across the amateur courts until she turned pro in 1926. Her opponents counted winning points, not games, as victories. She was beaten just once during that time, when she had to concede a match to Molla Mallory at Forest Hills in 1921 because, she claimed, of ill health.

Suzanne ruled the courts imperiously — once even keeping Queen Mary of England waiting and then finally refusing to play. She had a tempestuous, fiery nature off court, but in tennis play she was coolly calculating. American champion Helen Wills called Lenglen's game "a work of art."

La Grande Dame Suzanne did more to interest the world in the game of women's tennis than any other player of the long-skirted era. Yet for all her prowess on the courts, this great athlete never enjoyed good health and in 1938, when only thirty-nine years old, she died of pernicious anemia.

*France's Suzanne Lenglen showed her ballerina-style tennis to 13,000 fans in New York's Madison Square Garden in 1926.*       UPI

# Wills to Win

## • HELEN WILLS

When Helen Wills was born in Center-ville, California, in 1906, there were no great tennis coaches to teach the game to women. So women watched men to learn how to play. When Helen first saw the great champion Billy Johnston lash out at the ball, she tried to imitate his power and accuracy.

"I shall never forget trying my first forehand drive," Helen said. "I was a little girl with pigtails flying, playing on one of the side courts at the Berkeley Tennis Club. I didn't intend to drive, because I didn't know anything about strokes and their names. But when my ball went over the net, I knew that I had discovered a new and satisfying way of hitting the ball."

Before Miss Wills ended her career in 1938, she had discovered strokes so effective that her record is still hard to believe. She won the Wimbledon singles eight times, and earned three doubles titles. She took seven U.S. singles titles and four doubles crowns. She played in ten Wightman Cup matches, winning eighteen out of twenty singles matches. She also became the only American woman to win an Olympic gold medal for singles play in tennis. Helen Wills won the two most important titles in women's tennis, the U.S. Nationals and Wimbledon, more times than any other woman in history.

When Helen was a little girl, she decided to play tennis only because her best friend, a boy, liked the game better than anything else. Helen's father, a sports-loving doctor, also enjoyed tennis, and he encouraged his daughter by playing with her often. On her fourteenth birthday, when Helen beat him for the first time, he rewarded her with a membership in the Berkeley Tennis Club. There she won her first championship, the Pacific Coast Juniors. At fifteen she won the national junior girls' title, and at sixteen she reached the U.S. finals at Forest Hills, only to be defeated by Molla Mallory, eight-time winner of the Nationals.

The following year, 1923, in the brand new horseshoe stadium at Forest Hills, she defeated Mrs. Mallory to become the youngest woman to capture the crown since May Sutton in 1904.

Although Helen Wills will forever be remembered as America's greatest tennis queen, she was also a woman of remark-

*Helen Wills, who won the U.S. Nationals and Wimbledon more often than any other woman in history, was also the proud possessor of a Phi Beta Kappa key for her outstanding work in college.*

able versatility. She was a brilliant student who worked long hours on her studies and often just squeezed her tennis practice between classes and homework assignments. Her major was art, and she was so talented that when she wrote her autobiography, *Tennis*, in 1928, she did all of the illustrations herself.

When Helen was graduated from college, her diligence was appropriately rewarded, "I found that I had won a prize in my studies, which I shall cherish always more (I fear I must admit) than any of my tennis prizes — a Phi Beta Kappa key — and when they pinned it over my fast-beating heart, I experienced one of the happiest moments of my life."

Whatever Helen Wills did she did wholeheartedly and with such intense preoccupation that her determination showed on her face. Her nickname, Little Miss Poker Face, reflected this extreme concentration. "When I play," she said, "I become entirely absorbed in the game. I love the feel of hitting the ball hard, the pleasure of a rally. . . . Anyone who really loves the game can hardly be blamed for becoming completely absorbed by it while in the fun of play."

Her tennis strategy was also the beginning of a new kind of tennis for women. "I aim for the all-round game," she said. "This means good net and backcourt play, development of all strokes — backhand, forehand, etc. In other words the player should be at home wherever she may be on the court."

Yet Helen Wills and the women of her day were not always at home on the court. It obviously troubled young Helen to be ridiculously impeded by the long skirts, sleeves, and stockings considered the only appropriate dress for women tennis players. She stripped for action on the courts by wearing sleeveless shirts, ballerina-length skirts, and finally no stockings at all. But this change in women's dress did not come about easily.

In 1927, when she first showed up at a Queen's Club tournament in London without the acceptable long stockings, she created a sensation. Letters to newspapers poured in from an irate public, demanding that she be rebuked. Editorials debated the subject, "Should the authorities permit uncovered calves?" The matter was settled by the traditional majority when more than half of the women entered in the tournament courageously appeared on the court bare-legged.

The following year, the first shorts appeared at Wimbledon without much fuss. Helen Wills had led the way. That year she wrote in her book, "Unquestionably the short-skirted, sleeveless dress and the sensible way of dressing on the court is responsible, almost more than anything else, for the great improvement that has been seen in the standard of present-day tennis for women."

American women owe much to Helen Wills. She left us with a new game of tennis, to be played comfortably. Moreover, she was a queen to Americans, to be worshiped and imitated for her very special qualities. She was beautiful for her wholesomeness (she did not drink or smoke), brilliant for her devotion to hard work, and talented, and she worked to develop and perfect her talent. She was this country's answer to royalty, our queen, idolized by all who saw or read about her.

# Grand Slammers, Big and Little

- **MAUREEN CONNOLLY**
- **MARGARET SMITH COURT**

When twelve-year-old Maureen Connolly was playing in her first Southwest Pacific tennis tournament in 1947, eight-time Wimbledon winner, Helen Wills, was watching from the side court. Maureen's coach, Eleanor "Teach" Tennant, asked Ms. Wills what she thought of her protégé's game. "That little girl will become the national champion in four years," said the famed tennis queen with certainty. "And possibly the world's champion as well."

Maureen was overwhelmed by the prediction. She had been playing tennis for only two years, and there were still times when she would rather play ball or ride a horse. Her coach, however, was convinced that through hard work and devotion to practice, Maureen could fulfill the prophecy. Teach's rules were rigid: no late hours or rich foods. There would be no time for the normal teen-age pursuits — parties, dances, other sports, or even listening to favorite bop records.

Tennis was no game to Ms. Tennant. It was a battlefield. She was the field marshal and Maureen was the soldier. Spurred on by an overwhelming need to win, the young player tackled her opponents with almost fierce hatred. "The tennis court became my secret jungle and I, a lonely, fear-stricken hunter," said Maureen. "I was a strange girl armed with hate, fear and a Golden Racket."

As the years progressed, the prophecy came true. At fourteen, Maureen played the tennis circuit for the first time and won fifty-six straight matches. She became the California junior champion and the youngest winner of the National Juniors. In 1951, when she was sixteen, just four years after Helen Wills had first watched her play, the 5 foot 3 inch "Little Mo" defeated Shirley Fry at Forest Hills in the U.S. Women's singles to become that tournament's youngest champion. She won the Nationals two more consecutive times and each of those years was voted Woman Athlete of the Year by the Associated Press.

In 1953, when Maureen was nineteen, she became the first woman in history to win all the world's major tennis tournaments — Wimbledon, French, Australian, and United States — a grand slam.

Tragically, Little Mo's competitive

In 1953, when Maureen Connolly was nineteen, she became the first woman in the world to win the four major tennis tournaments in one year–Wimbledon (British), French, Australian, and U.S.–a grand slam. UPI

Australia's Margaret Smith Court won more than sixty major tournaments, including a grand slam in 1970. UPI

years ended prematurely. The following year her leg was permanently injured in a horseback-riding accident, and she eventually settled down to making a home for her husband Norman Brinker and their two children. But even this career was cut short. Early in 1969, when she was thirty-four years, little Mo died of cancer.

A year later, Australia's queen tennis player, Margaret Smith Court, became the world's second grand slammer — her accomplishment capped by her defeat of Billie Jean King in a record forty-six-game final at Wimbledon.

Margaret's first international triumph came in 1962, when she was twenty-four and won her first U.S. singles title. After adding Wimbledon to her credit, she retired to marry Barry Court and raise a family. But Barry was not content to have his talented wife give up her career, and with

him as her manager Margaret made a comeback. The family was a common sight on the circuit, Margaret, Barry, and "Nanny" — with the children, Danny and Marika, in tow.

By 1973, the statuesque 5 foot 9 inch Ms. Court was being hailed as the wonder woman of tennis. She was the greatest woman player to come out from down under — a country that produced more tennis superstars than any other. She had piled up a record of sixty-one major titles, including Wimbledon three times and the U.S. Nationals five times. That year she played the Virginia Slims circuit and won the trophy for making the most points. She was also the tour's top prize money winner — earning $180,058!

Margaret had proved that motherhood needn't stand in the way of a determined athlete.

# On Court in Black and White

## • ALTHEA GIBSON

In 1927, when Althea Gibson was born in Silver, South Carolina, there were few blacks, male or female, who had achieved fame in the sports world. The bigoted white community had made it virtually impossible for a black athlete to rise to star status.

Born into this type of society, a young black girl would have to have extraordinary strength of purpose, superior skill in sport, and a hardened ability to take insult and abuse in order to reach the top.

Althea Gibson was such a girl. She was too young to remember her earliest days on a southern cotton farm, but her growing-up years on the slum streets of Harlem, New York City's black ghetto, were vividly etched on her mind. These beginnings made Althea the fighter she was and gave her the compelling drive to find her place in the sun.

At home, in school, and on the streets, young Althea fought a constant battle for survival and identity. She knew she must find a way out of the city jungle. "I always wanted to be somebody," she said in her autobiography. "I was determined to be somebody if it killed me."

But how? How could this black girl, defiant of authority, disinterested in school, wild and undisciplined, find her way out of the ghetto? When she won the New York City paddle-tennis championship in 1939, she realized that sports could be her answer. And fortunately, there were others in a position to help her.

There was a recreation leader who recognized her special athletic skills, a tennis club that extended membership to her, a tennis pro who gave her free lessons, and most important a wealthy black doctor who took her into his home when she was nineteen and encouraged her to continue her education while concentrating on playing tennis. Dr. Hubert Eaton, Althea's sponsor, believed she had the makings of a great player and offered to pay all her living and training expenses.

In Wilmington, North Carolina, where Althea lived with the Eaton family, she felt the sting of southern segregation for the first time. "Colored in the Rear," "Whites Only," "No Blacks Allowed" appeared on signs everywhere. The Civil Rights Act of 1964 had not yet been passed, and "equal but separate" was still a way of life in the

*Althea Gibson at Wimbledon.*

South. Unable to play on the public courts, she practiced daily on the Eatons' backyard tennis court. When she had no partners she played against a Tom Stroke Developer — a robot machine that fired balls across the net at her.

Before long Althea was winning all the American Tennis Association tournaments. The ATA was the Negro tennis circuit, and when Althea won their national women's championship in 1947, she felt she had gone as far as she could. No blacks had ever played on the white circuit and she did not think of herself as a crusader for civil rights.

But Dr. Eaton thought otherwise, and he asked Althea the most important question of her life: "How would you like to play at Forest Hills?" Because of her special qualities the astonished young woman could give only one answer, "I'm ready," she replied, "anytime they are."

Early in 1950, when she was twenty-three, Althea became the first black to play in the Eastern and National Indoor tournaments. But as the summer drew closer there was still no invitation to play in the Nationals at Forest Hills, New York. It looked as though the United States Lawn Tennis Association would keep its doors barred. Then, in the July issue of *American Lawn Tennis* magazine there appeared a plea from a past National

champion — Alice Marble: "If Althea Gibson represents a challenge to the present crop of players," she wrote, "then it's only fair that they meet this challenge on the courts."

Several weeks later, in mid-August, the USLTA met its challenge and Althea Gibson became the first black to play in the traditionally all-white tournament. Although she did not win the championship, her very presence in the Forest Hills stadium was a stirring sight. Dave Eisenberg of the New York *Journal American* wrote, "I have sat in on many dramatic moments in sports, but few more thrilling than Miss Gibson's performance . . . not because great tennis was played but because of the great try by this lonely and nervous Negro girl. . . ."

But Althea did go on to play great tennis. In 1957 she defeated Darlene Hard at Wimbledon to win the British championship and then returned to Forest Hills to win the U.S. Nationals that year and again in 1958. Those years she was the winner of the Associated Press Woman Athlete of the Year award — the only black so honored.

At Wimbledon Althea Gibson, once a Harlem urchin, shook hands with the queen of England and received a congratulatory letter from President Eisenhower. Althea's triumph was not only a personal victory, but also a national one for believers in democracy. The London *Evening Standard* eloquently summed it up in an editorial:

> More than the Negro people should benefit from Miss Gibson's victory. . . . It further underlines the willingness of the British to take to their hearts those of any race, creed, or color. And it shows that somewhere in the great American dream there is a place for black as well as white. . . .

# From Down Under to the Top

## • EVONNE GOOLAGONG

Evonne Goolagong grew up several hundred miles from the nearest big city in the vast, dry, uninteresting sheep country of Barellan, Australia. She was descended from the original Aborigines of Australia, who, like our own American Indians, had been low on the social ladder and treated with scorn and prejudice. Tennis was an exclusive game played by and for the wealthy whites, and for a native Australian to rise to fame in that sport was an even greater triumph.

Mr. Goolagong was an itinerant fruit picker and sheep shearer, and providing for his wife and seven children was not easy. Although Evonne described her house as the "worst in town" and although the Goolagongs were the only "dark people" out of a population of nine hundred, Evonne was a happy child and grew up as all country children did — searching for swans' eggs, fishing for yabbies (a kind of crayfish), and playing outdoors. Her games were rugby, cricket, and soccer with the neighborhood boys.

In 1953, when Evonne was two, four well-lighted, red-loam tennis courts were erected in Barellan through funds raised in honor of the town's dead servicemen. Membership in the War Memorial Club was only $4 a year, and it fast became the hub of the social life in the quiet farm community. A summer tennis school under the jurisdiction of VAETS (Victor A. Edwards Tennis Schools) was established and when Evonne was eight years old she started taking lessons. She was an exceptional player, and for the next five years she competed in small country tournaments in places with names like Cootamundra, Wagga Wagga, and Yanco. However, it soon became evident that if Evonne was to make it to the top, she would have to go to Sydney, the seat of the Australian tennis world.

The Goolagongs obviously could not afford to sponsor their daughter in a tennis career, but she was good enough to become the protégé of Victor Edwards himself. He invited the young girl to live with him and his family in Sydney while she went to school and played in the age-group tournaments. Two of Mr. Edwards's daughters, Patricia and Jennifer, admitted many years later, that when they learned that Evonne would live with them, they pictured an Aborigine stereotype . . . a dark girl wearing a loin cloth and carrying a spear in one hand and a boomerang in the other!

With a racket in hand, however, Evonne quickly dispelled this idea. The Edwards family was charmed by the warm, outgoing disposition of this un-spoiled girl. She soon became a much-loved member of the household. Mr. Edwards became her coach, trainer, and manager; and as the years went on, he also became her legal guardian and surrogate parent. How well he did his job was reflected in the long list of Evonne's attributes. She was "everybody's darling" — the sunshine girl — warm, lively, graceful, carefree, and good-natured. And how she could play tennis!

In 1971, when she was twenty years old, she became only the second Australian woman to win at Wimbledon. She defeated her idol and countrywoman, Margaret Court. After being ranked number one that year, she was the Associated Press's choice for Woman Athlete of the Year. The following year, she was chosen Australian of the Year and Athlete of the World (U.S. Press Association choice), and her name was entered on the queen of England's honors list.

On the professional circuit, Evonne was a big winner, too. Her finest hour came in the Virginia Slims tournament of 1974. She entered the tournament seeded number one and winner of the championships in Italy, France, and Great Britain. Going into the Slims' final in Los Angeles, Evonne had a 36–3 record. She had just defeated Billie Jean King in the semis, and before a crowd of 7,049 she trounced Chrissie Evert in straight sets. She walked away with a unprecedented prize of $32,000.

Evonne Goolagong, a unique player, has always played with joy. Her love of the fun of the game can be seen in the radiant way she has competed. Goolagong — the melodious word means tall trees by still waters — is an Aborigine name. "I love my name," Evonne says. "Secretly, it is the thing about me I like best." Such modesty is typical of this remarkable tennis player from "down under."

*Evonne Goolagong, whose aborigine name means "tall trees by still waters," defeated her idol and countrywoman Margaret Court at Wimbledon in 1972 to become number one in the world.*

UPI

# The King Who Was Queen

## • BILLIE JEAN KING

In New York, London, Paris, Rome — in all of the large cities and some of the small ones around the world — newspapers on the morning of July 7, 1975, carried stories echoing the headline "And the King is Still Queen."

The King was Billie Jean King, who had just won her sixth Wimbledon singles title by defeating Australia's Evonne Goolagong Cawley in a quick and easy thirty-nine-minute match, 6–0, 6–1. Nine years earlier, Ms. King had taken a triple victory on the same hallowed British courts — the singles, doubles, and mixed-doubles championships. It was also recorded that Billie Jean now shared the record of nineteen Wimbledon titles with America's Elizabeth Ryan, who had won all of hers in the 1920s and '30s as a doubles player. This 1975 win brought mixed emotions because thirty-one-year-old Ms. King had previously announced that this would be her last major singles tournament.

As a youngster, Billie Jean Moffitt was an ace at softball, not tennis. Her father, an engineer with the Long Beach, California, fire department, considered baseball an unladylike sport. "So I convinced her she should try something else," he said. "I enrolled her in the city's free tennis training program and she did the rest."

When she was twelve, only a year after picking up a tennis racket, Billie Jean won her first tournament. There was no stopping her after that. She played tennis every day during the summer, after school, and on weekends. Neither Mr. or Mrs. Moffitt played tennis and Billie Jean's new-found love for the sport came as a surprise. "She just talked about wanting to be a champion. She said there wasn't anything more in the world she wanted than to play someday at Wimbledon," said her dad.

When she was sixteen, "Jillie Bean" as she was called, was ranked nineteenth in the country, which was an accomplishment for a youngster who had been playing only four years. At that point her training began in earnest. Her teacher was former Wimbledon and United States champion Alice Marble, who was a coach and tennis club owner in Palm Springs, California. Miss Marble invited Billie Jean to stay with her on weekends.

*Superstar Billie Jean King, winner of six Wimbledon singles titles, upheld her position as a fighter for the rights of women athletes when she defeated Bobby Riggs at the "Match of the Century" in 1973.*     WIDE WORLD

"She was so crazy about tennis, I'd have to lock her in her room to do her homework," said the coach of her new pupil. When Billie Jean played tennis, however, she needed no encouragement to work. Miss Marble changed her whole game around, took it apart, and put it back together again.

Poor Billie Jean was also put on a strict diet — no more ice cream, her favorite treat — and was kept in shape off the courts by running and skipping rope. All the hours of practice and self-discipline paid off. When Alice Marble finished with her, only six months later, Billie Jean's 1960 rank had jumped from nineteenth to fourth!

Billie Jean went to Wimbledon for the first time in 1961, when she was seven-teen, and won her first title there playing doubles with Karen Hantze. The following year in the opening round of singles play, she created quite a sensation when she defeated the favored top-ranking world player, Margaret Smith (later Margaret Court). Although she did not win the tournament that year, she won an unexpected share of British fans, who dubbed her "Little Miss Moffitt." A delightful young lady, with an expressive face, Billie Jean was vivacious and talkative, and the crowds adored her. "The crowd helped me a great deal — if the underdog makes a point, everyone claps, and, boy, you just go," she told reporters after the match.

Billie Jean's sense of humor made her one of the most popular players on the circuit. In 1965, when she married Larry

King, a law student at the University of California at Berkeley, she quipped, "All that running and skipping was useful. I met Larry at California State College where I was studying, and he chased me till I caught him."

Her partnership with Larry led to new goals in the career of this star athlete. In April, 1968, after naming her husband as her business manager, Billie Jean started on the professional trail. Her contract, as announced by George MacCall, president of the National Tennis League, "was in the neighborhood of $40,000 to $50,000 and could increase to $70,000 through tournament victories."

In the years that followed she became a leader in the fight for greater financial recognition for women athletes. She outspokenly demanded prize monies and endorsements more equal to those awarded to men. By the fall of 1971, Billie Jean had become the first woman athlete to earn $100,000 in a single year. She continued to carry her cause across the country by playing superb tennis in such commercially sponsored ventures as World Team Tennis, and the Virginia Slims and L'eggs World Series tournaments. She and Larry even published their own magazine to meet the needs of women athletes . . . womenSports.

Billie Jean played a hard, fierce, aggressive game. As one sports writer commented, "She buzzes the net like a torpedo approaching for the blast." She had impressed even the most skeptical males. Billie Jean King became the only woman athlete to be honored by *Sports Illustrated* magazine, when they named her Sportswoman of the Year at their usual annual Sportsman award.

There was one man, however, who still brazenly expressed disdain for women's tennis. Former National champion Bobby Riggs, now labeled chief of the "male chauvinist pigs," challenged Ms. King to the Match of the Century at the Houston Astrodome on September 20, 1973.

The event had all the trappings of a circus. A parade accompanied by the music of hundreds of musicians preceded the game. There were marchers dressed up as skunks and elephants, and marchers dressed down as gladiators, Tarzans, and dancing girls. In the audience, *Sports Illustrated* reported, were "hardhats and hippies, libbers and lobbers, chauvinists and charlatans." Billie Jean was carried onto the court in an Egyptian litter; Riggs in a Chinese rickshaw. He presented her with an all-week caramel sucker; she gave him a live baby pig with a pink bow.

Although it all seemed like good fun, the match was fought in deadly earnest. Ms. King won, 6–4, 6–3, 6–3. Women athletes all over the world cheered in unison for their queen and leader.

# For Love and Money

## • CHRIS EVERT

When sixteen-year-old Chrissie Evert entered room 101 at St. Thomas Aquinas High School on the morning of September 13, 1971, she looked like every other co-ed in her eleventh grade homeroom. She wore a green plaid skirt and white blouse, and her long, light hair hung straight over her shoulders.

But she wasn't simply another co-ed. Everyone in her Ft. Lauderdale school — in fact most everyone in the whole state of Florida — had avidly followed the news about their home-grown tennis champion, who had captured the heart of the sports world at her first U.S. Open Tennis tournament at Forest Hills, New York. Her proud and exuberant classmates crowded around her as she entered the class — two weeks late for school.

Chrissie had come from a season on the tennis circuit (forty-six straight singles victories since February) climaxed by reaching the semifinals at Forest Hills. There she had volleyed her way past such top-seeded performers as France's Françoise Durr and into the clutches of the number one women's player, Billie Jean King. Although the teen-ager lost that match, she

came out as the unquestioned darling of the tennis world. And, as an even greater plum, Chris was invited to become a member of the Wightman Cup team, which made her the youngest competitor since Maureen Connolly to be accorded that honor.

Chris Evert's emergence on the tennis scene in 1971 was hardly a surprise to her family. The Everts were all top-notch players. Her father and coach, Jim, taught the sport on the municipal courts of the Holiday Park Tennis Center in Lauderdale. Her older brother, Drew, at eighteen, was the third ranking Florida junior. Fourteen-year-old Jeannie was number one nationally in the fourteen-and-under group; ten-year-old John ranked ninth in the twelve-and-under group; and in October, 1975, the baby of the family, Clare, entered her first tournament when she was only seven years old.

Chris, too, began to play early; her father gave her a racket when she was five years of age. As she got older, he set up a rigorous practice schedule for her and saw to it that she was entered in almost every age-group tournament available. She was runner-up in the twelve-year-olds and won the fourteens and sixteens before making her debut at Forest Hills and emerging as the youngest woman to reach the semifinals there.

After that, there was no stopping Chris. When she was seventeen she won the richest women's tennis tournament of the time — the $100,000 Virginia Slims Championship at Boca Raton, Florida. Her defeat of Australian pro Kerry Melville in the finals should have meant $25,000 for her, but the U.S. Lawn Tennis Association would not allow her to accept any money as a tennis player until she was eighteen.

In the short time Chris had been in big-league competition she had protected herself with a mental shield that was at once the envy and the dislike of many older, more experienced players. Chris was a "cool one," who drew huge crowds to her matches. Yet the spectators were often hostile to her because of her aloofness and seemingly unimpassioned, mechanical brand of tennis. But friendly or not, the fans came to see the "ice princess" win. And she did not disappoint them.

As she entered her eighteenth year, her first as a pro, there was no doubt that she was among the world's greatest tennis players. Chris won six out of seven tournaments — and $41,000 — during the 1973 season. In 1974 her wins included the French, Canadian, and Wimbledon championships along with a dozen other tournaments. She also captured another prize, the heart of top-seeded twenty-one-year-old Jimmy Connors. Their on-again, off-again romance was the talk of the sports pages during the years that followed. In those years, the ice began to melt and Chris appeared to emerge as a warmer, wiser young woman.

In 1975, still before her twenty-first birthday, Chris and Jimmy were each ranked first in tennis and reigned king and queen. Chris started the season as the overwhelming choice of the Associated Press in the 1974 Woman Athlete of the Year selection. Before 1975 was over she had amassed over $400,000 in tournament monies and endorsements and had rolled up a streak of seventy-six clay-court victories. Her crowning achievement was when she returned to Forest Hills to defeat Evonne Goolagong, 5–7, 6–4, 6–2, for her first U.S. Open title.

In a span of four years Chris Evert had been loved, envied, hated, and admired. She may have left behind the carefree days of her teens, but on the way she had acquired skill, power, wealth, and maturity. The princess had truly grown into a queen.

*Chrissie Evert, chosen 1974 Woman Athlete of the Year, ran up a streak of seventy-six clay-court victories climaxed by her first U.S. open at Forest Hills in 1975.*   UPI

# TRACK AND FIELD

## The Ageless Racer

### • STELLA WALSH

Stella Walsh, a nineteen-year-old sprinter from Cleveland, Ohio, stunned 16,000 Madison Square Garden fans in 1930 by running the 50-yard dash in a world-record-breaking time of 6.1 seconds. She was competing in the usually all-male Millrose Games held annually in this famous New York City arena. To top the evening, Stella was named the "outstanding performer" of the meet.

Stella Walsh was born Stanislawa Walasiewicz in Poland in 1911. She came to America in her mother's arms when she was ten months old. She claimed to have spent her childhood running in the streets, playgrounds, and high school gymnasiums. "I don't think I ever walked," she said.

Stella was raised in an athletic family. Her mother and maternal grandfather loved sports and encouraged her physical activities. On a visit to Poland when she was in her teens, her grandfather, then seventy years old, challenged his "whippersnapper" granddaughter to a race around the family farm. "He really showed me a thing or two," recalled Stella, admiring his stamina.

Following her success in the Millrose games, Stella went on to become U.S. outdoor champion in the 100-meter dash (four times), the 200-meter dash (eleven times), the broad jump (ten times), indoor champion at 220 yards (six times), and 50 yards (twice). All told she won forty U.S. championships and an Olympic gold medal for Poland in the 1932 Olympics at Los Angeles when she was not yet an American citizen. Her gold medal 100-meter performance at 11.9 seconds was a world record. Sports writers claimed she had the nearest thing to a man's stride they had ever seen.

But it wasn't her collection of records and medals alone that made Stella Walsh one of the world's great athletes. It was her ability to sustain her racing skills over a long period of time. Stella won her first U.S. championship in 1930 (100-meter dash) when she was nineteen, and eighteen years later she won that same championship for the fourth time. In 1953, twenty-three years after her first victory, she was still in major competition. At forty-two years of age, she entered the western regional meet of the Women's National AAU pentathlon and won the five-event competition with a record-breaking performance.

Stella Walsh had turned back the clock and added another milestone to the accomplishments of women athletes.

*Polish-born Stella Walsh won the first of her forty U.S. track championships in 1930, and her last twenty-three years later, when she was forty-two years old.*

# The Flying Housewife

## • FANNY BLANKERS-KOEN

Her pictures appeared in the local Dutch newspapers: bicycling to practice sessions with her two little children propped in the basket strapped to the rear wheel, high jumping in the field while her youngsters played in the sandpit nearby, sitting on the grass strip in the middle of the cinder track and darning her husband's socks while waiting for her turn at the mark. Such domestic scenes seemed improbable in the midst of the all-out physical efforts that usually accompanied preparing for the Olympic Games.

Yet, here was twenty-nine-year-old Francina (Fanny) Blankers-Koen of the Netherlands, known throughout Europe as the "flying housewife," training for the 1948 Olympics to be held in London that summer. Her nickname was given her out of affection, and in admiration for her skill in track events, rather than because of male chauvinist notions. She was loved because she represented the spirit and unity of family life, which had been disrupted during the long, horror-filled years of World War II. Completing this family picture was the fact that Fanny's coach was her husband Jan Blankers.

Fanny's career began in 1935, when she was sixteen. She had been a very good swimmer but her local instructor suggested she switch to track. "Holland already has a surplus of swimming stars," he advised, and she followed his suggestion. Within a year, Fanny had qualified for her country's Olympic team, and at the Berlin Games in 1936 she placed sixth in the high jump.

Because of the War, the Olympics were not held in 1940 and 1944, but in 1948 more than six thousand athletes from every major country except Russia, Germany, and Japan prepared to resume peacetime athletic encounters. After arranging for their children to stay with her father, Fanny and Jan joined their teammates on the trip to the Olympic Games in London.

Fanny was entered in five events: the 100- and 200-meter dashes, the 80-meter hurdles, the 400-meter relay, and the long jump. In her first event, the 100 meters, despite a cold stinging rain, Fanny flew past her closest opponent, Dorothy Manley of Great Britain. The strains of the "Wilhelmus," the Dutch national anthem,

*Fabulous Fanny Blankers-Koen, mother of two, won four gold medals for Holland in the 1948 Olympic Games in London.*                                                                  UPI

rang out in the London stadium and Fanny had her first gold medal.

Now she faced the 80-meter hurdles and a rival who was ten years younger than she, Maureen Gardner, a pretty ballet teacher from London. Because of the confusion caused by a misfiring starting pistol, Fanny got a late start, but somehow managed to catch up by the last hurdle. As she felt the tape across her chest, she heard the crowd roaring with excitement. They were watching what seemed to be a triple dead heat — Ms. Gardner and Shirley Strickland from Australia were head to head with Fanny. While the judges studied the photo-finish, the band started to play "God Save The King" and Fanny concluded that Ms. Gardner had won. But the music was saluting the arrival of King George in the royal box. A few seconds later, the sounds of "Wilhelmus" echoed through the arena, once more indicating a gold medal for Fanny Blankers.

Ahead lay the 200-meter event, which in 1948 was the longest race for women in the Olympics. Again in a driving rain, this time leaving her closest opponent far behind, fabulous Fanny took first place. Then with the help of her Dutch teammates, she anchored the 400-meter relay, to bring back to Amsterdam her fourth gold medal.

The Hollanders honored Fanny by naming a candy bar, a gladiolus, and a rose after her. They paraded her through the streets in an open coach drawn by four white horses. The most outstanding track and field athlete of her time, the flying housewife had flown farther and faster than her countrymen dreamed possible.

# Master of the Discus

## •OLGA FIKOTOVA CONNOLLY

When Olga Fikotova won the gold medal for her discus throw in the 1956 Olympics, her country, Czechoslovakia, honored her with the title of "supreme master of sports" — the highest designation a Czech athlete can achieve. She became a national celebrity.

A career in sports was a popular and much respected way of life for a Czechoslovakian woman. With a gold medal around her neck, Olga looked forward to many more years as a sports star. But before the Games were over, her plans began to change dramatically. She met and fell in love with Harold Connolly, the American gold medalist in the 16-pound hammer throw.

After several soul-searching months apart, Olga and Hal decided to get married, and Olga left her home for a new one in America. Her life would be with a man of a different background, education, and religion. She would live in a Western democratic country that opposed the communist government then in control of her native Czechoslovakia.

The wedding was heralded in a New York Times editorial on March 22, 1957. It read:

> This poor old world of ours is quarreling, divided and perplexed. . . . The H-bomb overhangs us like a cloud of doom . . . but Olga and Harold are in love and the world does not say no to them. . . . Somehow this seems like a ray of light, intelligence and beauty in a world where ministers of state and heads of government go nervously back and forth in search of such things. . . .

Olga found American attitudes toward women athletes very different from those of Europeans. In New England, where she and Harold set up their first home, she was amazed at the still prudish outlook toward women in competitive sports. Once, after encouraging a group of young girls at a high school assembly program to go out for some of the more strenuous field events, she was criticized by the school principal. "The hands of our girls are created to play violin," he said. "Please do not put ideas in their heads about competition."

Olga answered angrily: "For seven years I played the violin and my hands were as good for that as for winning the Olympic Games."

It didn't take the new Mrs. Connolly long to realize that she would have a hard time staying at the top of world-class competition. "The meets in the United States are organized against local competition; major events are very scarce," she complained. "The schools are making every effort to keep hard exercise and competition out of the curriculums. They want to keep American women feminine, they say."

In spite of this and other obstacles — adjusting to a new way of life, keeping house, going to school, working part time — Olga Connolly, after first becoming a naturalized citizen of the United States, qualified for the Olympic teams four times, beginning in 1960. Between each of the Games, she was pregnant.

When she and Harold went to Munich in 1972, they were the parents of four children, a record for a competing woman Olympian. Olga was thirty-nine years old and still a master of the discus as well. She was the American standard holder at the 185 foot 3 inch mark.

*Olga Fikotova won an Olympic gold medal for Czechoslovakia in 1956 before coming to the United States to marry hammer-thrower Hal Connolly and qualify for four more Olympic Games.*

UPI

# Women Who Put the Shot

- **MARIANNE ADAM**
- **EARLENE BROWN**
- **NADYEZHDA CHIZHOVA**
- **HELENA FIBINGEROVA**
- **MICHELINE OSTERMEYER**
- **TAMARA PRESS**
- **MAREN SEIDLER**

"I hope sports will begin to lose its sex definition of shot-putting as a male sport," said Maren Seidler, United States national champion shot-putter. "With proper training and dedication, a woman can do anything she sets out to achieve."

Certainly such athletes as Earlene Brown from the United States and Micheline Ostermeyer of France, as well as the nationally subsidized athletes from East Germany, Czechoslovakia, and the Soviet Union, have proved the truth of Maren Seidler's convictions.

The shot put has been an Olympic event for women only since 1948. "To put the shot" means to propel a small but heavy metal ball as far as the competitor can throw. For women, the ball, known as the shot, weighs 8 pounds 13⁴/₅ ounces, which is a little more than half of the regulation weight of the shot used by men.

Through the years of competition, women's skill in the sport has constantly improved as the athletes and their coaches have developed new and better ways of training. In 1948 the first Olympic winner, Micheline Ostermeyer put the shot at 45 feet 1½ inches. The world's record set in 1975 by Marianne Adam of East Germany was 70 feet 10½ inches!

In the United States the first Olympic medalist was Earlene Brown, who represented America three times in the Games, winning a bronze medal in 1960 with a throw of 53 feet 10⅜ inches. A versatile athlete, Earlene, who was twenty-five years old at the time, also took sixth place in the discus throw. When Earlene left amateur sports, she became a superstar in the Roller Derby, a fast-moving, hard-knocking, commercial American game on roller skates.

Maren Seidler put her first shot in 1966 at a meet in South Carolina when she was thirteen. To everyone's amazement, she broke her age-group national record when she threw the 6-pound shot 6 feet farther than anyone else. That success was what caused her to train seriously for a sport so rarely tackled by women in this country. In 1974, Maren set the American record at 56 feet 7 inches.

In all competitive sports proper coaching and training are the most important parts of an athlete's development. In the shot put, sprinting and weight lifting are

Maren Seidler set the American shot-put record at 56 feet 7 inches in 1974. *UPI*

Russia's versatile Tamara Press won the shot-put at the 1960 Olympics, and in 1964 was victorious in both the shot-put and the discus events. *UPI*

*Earlene Brown, eight-time national champion shot putter, won a bronze medal in the Rome Olympics in 1960.* WIDE WORLD

the major techniques needed for a good throw. In East Germany, Czechoslovakia, and Russia, a sports-training program starts for children at five years of age. Every youngster has a chart showing progress in both academic and physical-fitness programs. Those children who show special skill in running, throwing, or jumping train during part of their school day. There is no doubt that such early encouragement helps to produce champions.

The exciting performances of Russia's Tamara Press, two-time Olympic gold medalist (1960, 1964), and Nadyezhda Chizhova, who set the world and Olympic records in 1972, surely help prove the point. And although Czechoslovakian Helena Fibingerova's 1974 world mark has already been surpassed by an East German, who can fail to be impressed by that 70 foot 9¼ inch heave!

# The Black Gazelle

## • WILMA RUDOLPH

"On your mark, get set — go!" The starter's gun resounded through the Olympic stadium and the runners were off. Trailing a little behind the pack on this stifling September day in Rome, 1960, was a 5 foot 11 inch, 132-pound Afro-American girl — long, lean, and graceful as a deer in flight.

Twenty-year-old Wilma Rudolph was striding longer and faster now. The gap between Wilma and the lead runner, Russia's Maria Itkina, was closing. At the halfway mark, 50 meters, Wilma forged ahead. Eleven seconds after the crack of the starter's gun, Wilma Rudolph snapped the finish-line tape 3 yards ahead of her nearest competitor. She had won the 100-meter dash and her first Olympic gold medal.

This was only the beginning of Wilma's race to fame. In the days that followed, this lovely young girl, sleek and graceful as a panther, ran off with two more gold medals. In the 200-meter dash she broke the Olympic record and in the team event, the 400-meter relay, she and her teammates set a world and Olympic mark. She was the first American woman athlete to win three gold medals in Olympic track and field.

Sixteen years earlier, when Wilma was a child in Clarksville, Tennessee, she had been unable to walk. After a siege of double pneumonia and scarlet fever, one leg had been left completely useless. Her mother, who had borne nineteen children, carried Wilma for weekly visits to a clinic in Nashville. There, Wilma received heat and water therapy to build up her shrunken muscles. At home, Wilma's brothers and sisters took turns massaging her legs.

For over two years, the child was confined to a chair or bed. All during those painful, unhappy days, Wilma never complained. "It didn't make her cross," her mother said. "The other children came and played with her while she sat in her chair."

At last, when she was about six, Wilma started to walk again with the help of specially made shoes. It didn't take her long to make up for those long years of immobility. She was soon playing basketball and running races as well as any of her more active friends.

When she was thirteen, she made the Clarksville High basketball team. During practice one day she dribbled the ball

*In 1960 Wilma Rudolph became the first American woman to win three gold medals in track and field at the same Olympic Games.* UPI

wildly down the court and fell in an ungraceful heap at the feet of her coach, Clinton Gray. "A 'skeeter," he said. "You buzz around like a regular mosquito — fast, little, and always in my way."

But 'Skeeter was not little or in her coach's way for long. At fifteen, she had already grown to her full 6 foot height, and was an all-state basketball player, scoring a school record of 803 points in twenty-five games. The track coach at Tennessee A & I State University, Ed Temple, recognized Wilma's potential as a runner. He encouraged Coach Gray to start a track team at Clarksville High so she could get the training and experience she needed.

In less than a year of high school competition, Wilma earned a berth on the U.S. Olympic team. In 1956, when she was sixteen years old, she went to Melbourne, Australia, for the Olympic games and helped the U.S. women's team win a bronze medal in the 400-meter relay.

Wilma returned home and enrolled at Tennessee A & I. There, her track training was intensified under the expert guidance of Coach Temple. His biggest concern was that skinny Wilma didn't eat enough to

sustain her during the rigorous training program. "She won't eat and when she does, it's junk — hamburgers and pop.

She also liked to sleep and was often late for practice. In desperation, the coach ruled that all latecomers would have to run an extra lap for every minute they were tardy. Wilma was cured the hard way when one morning she arrived half an hour late. She had to run the extra 30 laps. One of her teammates, Martha Hudson, said of her, "I guess Wilma would rather sleep than do most anything. Next to that it's reading, but mostly in bed."

It's certain, however, from her record, that sleep did not slow down Wilma Rudolph. Spurred on by a superior group of teammates at Tennessee A & I, Wilma's speed earned her a reputation as "America's fastest woman."

"She's great," said her coach, "but she couldn't have done it alone. Her teammates are the next three fastest girls in the country. Barbara Jones ran a world record one hundred yards in ten point three seconds at Randalls Island, New York, in nineteen fifty-eight. Lucinda Williams and Martha Hudson also gave her a run for her money. Rudolph runs so fast because she is pressed so hard in practice. Without it, she wouldn't be nearly as good as she is."

This unusual team won six gold medals among them in the 1960 Olympics. After the games, Coach Temple (who was also an Olympic track coach) took his girls on tour, where they raced on tracks all over the world — in Athens, Amsterdam, London, Cologne, and Berlin. Wherever they went, the crowds besieged them.

Wilma was a cheerful heroine, beloved by everyone. In France they called her *La Perle Noire* (The Black Pearl); in Italy, *La Gazelle Nera* (The Black Gazelle). Back home in America, she was still known as

Skeeter — a darting, buzzing, wisp of a mosquito — the only American to win three gold medals in track and field in the same Olympic Games.

In a crowning tribute to Wilma, the Amateur Athletic Union in 1961 awarded her the Sullivan Memorial Trophy for her outstanding performance as an amateur athlete. Only two other women before her in the more than twenty-five-year history of the trophy had received this treasured prize. The inscription on the trophy reads: "To the athlete, male or female, who by performance, example and good influence did the most to advance the cause of good sportsmanship."

*Graceful Wilma Rudolph won the anchor leg in the 400-meter relay to give the track team a world record time of 44.5 seconds at the Rome Olympics in 1960.*

UPI

# Sprinting for the Love of It

## • WYOMIA TYUS SIMBERG

Standing in front of her track team at Beverly Hills High School, the coach tried earnestly to make a point. "Try to remember," she said, "that sports is and will be only one part of your life, not all of it. When you're running against your best friend, don't forget that you're both human beings first. It's good for women to be in the world of competitive sport so long as they don't get hung up on winning all the time."

What an unexpected lesson to be giving a female team in 1975 — a year of tennis "libber" Billie Jean King, the first women's basketball game in Madison Square Garden, *Ms. Magazine*, and the fight for passage of the women's Equal Rights Amendment. But Wyomia Tyus, the coach, was an unusual athlete, who despite her very sincere philosophy of running for fun, had done quite a lot of winning herself, as the decade's best woman sprinter.

Wyomia was born in 1945 on a dairy farm in Griffin, Georgia. The only girl in a family with three boys, she developed naturally into a good runner. She wasn't particularly outstanding in other sports,

but did make her high school track team. At a state-wide meet in 1961, Wyomia's natural, easy stride was spotted by Ed Temple, the noted track coach from Tennessee State. He asked her to join his special summer session and when she was graduated from high school in 1963, she accepted an athletic scholarship to Tennessee State.

Although Wyomia was a sprinter, she enrolled in a cross-country track course, which was supposed to be excellent conditioning for all athletes. In addition to running regular laps, students had to run 6 additional miles every day. As a first-year runner, without much experience in organized competition, Wyomia didn't even dream about such things as Olympics. Yet, with her natural ability, excellent training, and love for the sport, she unexpectedly made the 1964 Olympic team. At the Tokyo Games, she surprised everyone by coming in first in the 100-meter event and aiding her teammates to win a silver medal in the 400-meter relay.

Back home, the new champion was urged to stop competing by her mother and aunts, who thought it was very "unladylike" for a girl to be an athlete. Foolishly they told her she'd develop big muscles in her legs and look like a man. But Wyomia ran anyway. She loved the sport, and nothing could stop her.

When she prepared to compete in the 1968 Olympics in Mexico City, she was warned about the "repeat jinx" — no sprinter in history had ever won two consecutive gold medals in the 100-meter dash. Once again, Wyomia did the unexpected. Not only did she break the tape in the event, but she also joined Margaret Bailes, Mildrette Netter, and Barbara Ferrel for a victory in the 400-meter relay.

However, Wyomia did not take her gold medals back to America. In a gesture of solidarity with her fellow black athletes, she donated the prizes to Tommy Smith and John Carlos, the champions who had publicly rejected their own awards in protest against the United States' treatment of its black athletes.

Voted the top female athlete in the world in 1968, Wyomia Tyus Simberg retired to family life until 1973, when the Professional International Track Association was formed. On tour she ran the 60-yard dash, the only women's event on the program. She came back not only for money, but also for love. "I never ran just to win," she said, "and I still don't. I run because I like it."

*When Wyomia Tyus breasted the tape in the 100-meter dash at the 1964 Olympics in Tokyo, she became the only sprinter in history to win two consecutive Olympic firsts in that event.* UPI

# Girl on the Run

## • FRANCIE LARRIEU

Francie Larrieu came into this world sixth in a line of nine children. It took a lot of running to keep up with her five brothers — especially Ron, who was an Olympian runner in 1964. Francie was always running — with, against, or away from some member of the family.

When she was thirteen, she read about the Junior Olympics on the back of a box of Wheaties and decided she'd like to compete in them. At her first race for the Cindergals, a teen-age track club in Santa Clara, California, she missed the start of the 220-yard dash because she wasn't sure the 220 was a race. Her angry coach made sure she was on the mark for the 660 — which she won with no difficulty. Now she was off and running.

Francie qualified for her first U.S. track team in 1969. Then sixteen, she was not much more than 5 feet tall, and she weighed a scant 100 pounds. She was everybody's darling. Unfortunately however, she didn't seem to have enough stamina and was always either sick or involved in some clumsy accident. For the next few years, she hardly competed at all.

Finally in March, 1972, her coach Augie Argabright talked her into racing in a 2½

miler, as support for his leading cross-country runner, Jackie Dixon. Much to everyone's surprise Francie managed to finish ahead of half of the pack of thirty-one of the best distance runners in the country. The race brought back her old spirit of competition. "It's coming back," she said, delighted, "but I'd better hurry if I'm going to make the Olympic team."

And hurry she did — running as much as 100 miles a week in training. She left the Cindergals to join the older, more seasoned Pacific Coast Club, where she was the only woman athlete and as such competed frequently, often on a very tight schedule.

One bleak Thursday in February, 1975, Francie flew from Los Angeles to Toronto to compete in the Toronto Star–Maple Leafs Indoor Games. When she left Canada the next day, she held the world's record in the 1500 meters. After traveling 3,500 miles during a sleepless day and night, she was on the run again in San Diego. This time she set the world record in the mile at 4:29 and broke her own record in the 1500 meters with a clocking of 4:09.8.

Sixteen days later, in Richmond, Virginia, during the U.S.–U.S.S.R. indoor meet, she surpassed her old mile-time, setting the record at 4:28.5. She looked ahead to the 1976 Olympics with confidence. Behind her were broken records in the mile, 2 mile, 100, 1500 and 3000 meters.

What made this twenty-two-year-old UCLA junior keep running? "I found out early," she said, "that I couldn't stand to be anything but first, even if it was just running down the block." And so Francie ran on.

*Twenty-two-year-old Francie Larrieu set world records for 1 and 2 miles in 1975.*

# The Agony of the Short-Distance Runner

## • CHI CHENG REEL

The roar of the fans was deafening. A tall, slim, Oriental girl, pushing herself to the limits of endurance, was stretching her legs toward the victory tape. With one last supreme effort, her graceful, rhythmic body reached the finish line first and she collapsed in a heap.

This was the way Chi Cheng ran in fifty-nine out of sixty races during the summer of 1969. Although running was the most important thing in her life, every stride she took in competition caused her untold agony. According to an old Oriental saying, a journey of a thousand miles begins with the first step, but for this victorious sprinter, every step seemed to be a thousand miles.

Actually Chi Cheng's first step in competition began when she was a junior high school freshman in Taiwan. She had never run in an official race before, but the long-legged student had been chosen by her classmates to represent them in a provincial meet. She had often demonstrated her speed in games the youngsters played in the rice fields around their native town of Hsinchu. Although Chi Cheng came in last in that provincial race, she discovered that she had a special skill in sprinting and began to train in earnest.

In 1962, when she was eighteen, American track and field coach Vince Reel went to Taiwan for the Asian Games. He was so impressed with the speed and potential of this lovely young racer that he convinced her to come to the United States and train with him for the 1964 Olympics in Tokyo.

Chi Cheng made it to the Olympics, representing her homeland, but she had trouble from the very start. In the 80-meter hurdles, she was running head-to-head with the leader, Russian star Galina Bystrova when she hit the fifth hurdle and felt something snap in her thigh. The pain was severe and this Olympics was over for Chi Cheng.

In spite of the injury, Chi was determined to keep training. In 1967 she underwent an operation on her knee, and in 1968 she pulled muscles in both legs. Still she managed to make it to the 1968 Olympics in Mexico City, where she placed third in the hurdles and seventh at 100 meters.

By the beginning of 1970, Chi's legs

finally healed and her incredible speed and talent burst forth. In the next seven months she set world records at 100 yards, 100 meters, 220 yards, and 200 meters. All told, she broke or equaled seven world marks and lost only one race until December, when she once again suffered from a bad knee plus the permanent complication of a snapping hip.

She was named Woman Athlete of the Year for 1970, but her competitive days were nearing an end. The pain of her injuries was so great she could hardly walk. In the hope of finding some relief she went home to Taiwan for surgery. Doctors removed 14 inches of muscle from her left thigh and 11 inches from the right. After fifty-two days in the hospital, the champion sprinter returned to America, not to run, but simply to learn to walk again.

Sadly, "the world's fastest woman" had to abandon her racing career. But spunky Chi Cheng found other hurdles to challenge her. With her husband and former coach, Vince Reel, she became co-track coach at Redlands University in Redlands, California, teaching other sprinters and hurdlers to follow in her footsteps.

Champion sprinter Chi Cheng, who broke or equaled seven world records in 1970, was forced to retire because of painful injuries.

UPI

# A Bittersweet Triumph

## • HEIDE ROSENDAHL ECKER

The crowd of more than 75,000 stood up and cheered wildly in the glass-topped steel Olympic track stadium in Munich, West Germany. It was Sunday, September 10th, 1972, the last day of Olympic Games in which the memory of the murder of eleven Israelis and a West German remains more vivid than the athletic feats.

Now here was a tumultuous outpouring of love and pride for Heidemarie Rosendahl, West Germany's winner of two gold medals and a silver in the tragedy-filled Games. Heide had just defeated East Germany's champion sprinter Renate Stecher in the last leg of the 400-meter relay, making a total of five victories in track and field for the host country. This was her crowning achievement, climaxing a career of ten years in international competition. She would soon retire to America as the wife of basketball star John Ecker.

Heide began competing when she was fourteen. Her father had been national champion in the discus three times, and it was expected that she too would become an accomplished athlete. The first event she trained for was the most difficult of all — the pentathlon — a five-sport event that included the 100- and 200-meter hurdles, the shot put, high jump, and long jump.

In 1966, under the tutelage of her first coach, Gerd Osenberg, Heide enrolled in one of Germany's special sports universities. The unique course of study at the Sport University of Cologne included, along with such academic subjects as education, psychology, anatomy, and physiology, treatment of sports injuries and proficiency in athletics.

In order to be graduated from this university, a student had to demonstrate superiority in his or her sport. Being superior wasn't easy. For example, to make an A in the long jump a woman would have to jump 16 feet 10 inches, and a man 20 feet 21 inches. In addition to developing superior skills in a sport, the student also had to know how to teach it. Heide taught for four years at Cologne after graduation. When she was considered ready for international competition, she was given a grant of $250 a month to cover her training and equipment expenses.

In 1970 Heide had a major success. At the World University Games in Turin, Italy, she set the women's long-jump re-

*All-around athlete Heide Rosendahl Ecker won a gold medal in the long jump, a silver in the pentathlon, and anchored her West German team to victory in the 400-meter relay at the Munich Olympics in 1972.* UPI

cord at 22 feet 5¼ inches. She had been a popular sports heroine in Germany, but now was considered the favorite for the 1972 Olympics in Munich.

The first day of the Games was a clear, sparkling one and Heide prepared for her first event, the long jump. She went 22 feet 3 inches, which was the longest jump of the day, giving West Germany its first gold medal.

The pentathlon was held on the weekend. In this five-event competition, the athletes don't win or lose in the usual sense. It is a matter of margin of win, which is recorded in points. Although Heide actually won three of the five events, Mary Peters of Great Britain won the total points, 4,801 to Heide's 4,791. The 10-point difference meant a silver medal for Heide.

Two days later, the world learned of the murder of the athletes in Olympic Village by a band of Palestinian terrorists. More than anything, the Germans had wished for a peaceful Games. The last time Germany had hosted an Olympics was in Berlin in 1936. Remembering those days was bitter, recalling the rise of Hitler, Naziism, and World War II. The Germans had wanted to erase the image of the past and now the whole world once again was witness to terror and murder.

It was not difficult to understand then, why on the last day of the 1972 Games, when twenty-four-year-old Heide Rosendahl anchored her team to victory in the 400-meter relay, thousands of spectators rose in unison. Some cheered and some cried, for it was indeed a bitter victory for Germany.

# "No Kids Allowed"

## • MARY DECKER

When the world first noticed Mary Decker she was fourteen years old, 5 feet tall, and weighed a scant 86 pounds. She barely came up to the shoulders of her competitors at the Russian-American track meet in Minsk in the Soviet Union. The year was 1973.

As Mary settled into the starting block for the 800-meter race on the second day of competition it was apparent that the American team had already lost the meet. Mary, her hair drawn tightly into ponytails, got a good start, but she hung back in fourth place until the stretch, when she suddenly pulled ahead. In a sudden burst of speed, she swept past Russia's 1972 Olympic silver medalist, Niele Sabaite, for victory with a 2:02.9 clocking.

The cheers were deafening — from both sides — and they continued to be for her, on the rest of the American tour in Italy and Senegal. The elflike runner was winning hearts and races.

It all started when Mary was eleven and won her first age-group competition. A year later the youngster came within eight seconds of the record for the 16-mile cross-country event. At thirteen she broke the world record for her age-group in the half-mile. By the time she was fifteen she had set indoor records at 800 meters (2:01.8), 880 yards (2:02.4), and 1000 yards (2:26.7).

Yet, for all this acclaim, Mary was a very normal Orange High School (near Los Angeles, California) sophomore. She bit her fingernails, plucked her eyebrows, took "driver-ed" and "home-ec." She liked spaghetti, Bit-O-Honey's, Hostess Ding-Dongs, boys, and sleeping late; she hated the braces on her teeth and being treated like a baby.

Mary had problems because of her size. When she was warming up for the Sunkist track meet in Los Angeles in January, 1974, an AAU track official approached her. "Sorry," he said leading Mary off the track. "The kids had their races in the afternoon."

Her coach, Don De Noon, led her back in time for the start of the 1000-yard event. Her brown eyes still full of tears, Mary raced off to set the world record.

*Five-foot Mary Decker was only fourteen years old when she competed in a Russian-American track meet in the Soviet Union in 1974 and came in first in the 800-meter race.*

# MARATHON RUNNING

## You've Run a Long Way, Baby

- **SARA MAE BERMAN**
- **ROBERTA GIBB BINGAY**
- **NINA KUSCSIK**
- **KATHY SWITZER MILLER**

It was a brisk April day in 1966 when the starter signaled the beginning of the sixty-ninth annual Boston Marathon. Run over a 26-mile, 385-yard course between Hopkinton and Boston, Massachusetts, this is the oldest and largest marathon in the United States and the only one in the country where more than 100,000 spectators line the course.

Running among the 415 starters was a graceful figure clad in a hooded sweatshirt. When the runner crossed the finish line ahead of 290 fellow competitors and pulled off the hooded jersey, it was apparent that a young blonde female had run in this traditionally all-male competition.

Mrs. Roberta Gibb Bingay, wife of a Tufts University distance runner, thus became the first woman to unofficially run in the Boston Marathon. "I was in it for the fun," she said, "but I also wanted to make people see something different that would shake them up a bit, and maybe even change some old-fashioned attitudes."

And, indeed, that's about all she achieved. The following year another woman ran the race, entered simply as K. Switzer, and again wearing a hooded disguise. Kathy Switzer, however, was discovered during the course of the race and an official tried to forcibly pull her out of the competition. The resulting publicity subsequently pressured Marathon officials into permitting women to run the course.

Sara Mae Berman, with a 3:05.07 clocking in 1970, is considered to have the

*Roberta Gibb Bingay rests after becoming the first woman to run in the 26-mile Boston Marathon in 1966.* UPI

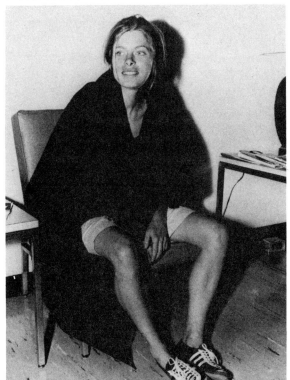

women's record, even though it was set before a women's division of the Boston Marathon was officially established in 1972.

That year, Nina Kuscsik adjusted the number F2 on her back and made ready for the start of the Boston race. Thirty-three-year-old Ms. Kuscsik, mother of three, was on an equal footing with such male entries as entertainer Dick Gregory; *Love Story* author, Erich Segal; six officers of the Los Angeles police force; her husband Dick, and 1,071 others. When Nina crossed the finish line with a time of 3:08:58, she finished ahead of 800 male racers and 8 other women to become the first woman champion of the Boston Marathon.

Before the big race, Ms. Kuscsik had commented: "Every runner in this race will have his or her own goal. . . . The greatest thing is that everyone can come out a winner by reaching that goal." Nina Kuscsik had reached her own personal goal by winning the race, but she also reached the common goal of women athletes everywhere. She had officially proved that women, like men, have the strength and determination to run long distances.

*Marathon runner Nina Kuscsik, mother of three, became the first winner of the women's division of the Boston Marathon in 1972.* UPI

*Kathy Switzer Miller, who ran in a hooded disguise in the 1967 Boston Marathon, raced in a fully recognized women's division in 1972 as a fully recognizable female.* UPI

# VOLLEYBALL

## Ms. Superstar

### • MARY JO PEPPLER

Volleyball, like baseball, is a home-grown American-made sport, and virtually everyone in America has played the game at one time or another. It is a sport for people of all ages, all sizes, all degrees of athletic ability, and for both men and women.

Yet, for all this universality, we do not usually associate volleyball with great athletes — male or female. That is what makes the story of Mary Jo Peppler so extraordinary.

When Mary Jo was growing up in the San Fernando Valley of California, she preferred playing with boys because she liked their rough and tumble kind of sports and the directness of their competitive spirit. But when she started playing quarterback on the neighborhood team, her parents put a stop to such boy-girl athletics. At that time, volleyball was considered primarily a healthy, social co-ed game, and so that became Mary Jo's favorite sport.

By her senior year in high school, in 1962, she was good enough to play for the women's national championship team, the Long Beach Shamrocks. Two years later, she helped form a new team, the Los Angeles Renegades, and like true renegades they captured the AAU national title. That year and again in 1968, Mary Jo played on the U.S. Olympic team, but both times the caliber of American athletes, coaches, and game strategy was a great disappointment to her. Her superiority on the court was universally accepted. In 1970 at the international games in Bulgaria, she was voted the best woman volleyball player in the world.

When she moved to Texas, she organized the E Pluribus Unum team of Houston, and under her gifted coaching, this powerful team took the AAU title away from the Renegades in 1972 and 1973. But Mary Jo was a "renegade" at heart, and in her overzealous desire to improve the quality of America's Olympic team, she ran into difficulties with the U.S. Volleyball Association. "She's a gifted athlete who can't be handled," said Al Monaco, executive director of the USVBA. She was told that she would not be needed, as a player or a coach, for the 1976 Olympic team. It was a bitter blow for an athlete who had dreamed of one day winning a gold medal.

Leaving her amateur status behind, Mary Jo turned all her efforts towards playing for the El Paso-Juarez team of the newly formed professional International Volleyball Association. The new pro team, like the other teams of the IVA consisted of four men and two women players, which made volleyball the first truly professional co-ed sport.

In January, 1975, still considered the best woman volleyball player in the world, thirty-year-old Ms. Peppler was thrust into the limelight in a most spectacular way. The magazines *Ladies Home Journal* and *womenSports* were sponsoring a super sports competition for women in Rotonda, Florida. The men had already found their superstar — football player O. J. Simpson — and now a selected group of athletes from all over the country competed in seven out of ten events to determine who would be Ms. Superstar.

Mary Jo chose basketball free-throw shooting, softball throwing, the 60- and 440-yard dashes, cycling, rowing, and swimming. The athletes were excluded from competing in their own specialty so that everyone would have an equal chance.

On the first day of competition, Mary Jo came in second in the bike race, fourth in the 60-yard sprint, and fifth in the 440 as well as the swimming event. It seemed like a poor showing and nobody had any great hopes for Mary Jo. The next day's competitions included the softball, basketball, and rowing events, all of which she won decisively.

When the points had been added and penalty points subtracted, the 6 foot, 155-pound Mary Jo had won the competition — 3 points ahead of basketball star Karen Logan and 5 points better than diver Micki King. The new women's superstar took home total winnings of $49,600, ten times more money than she had earned in volleyball the year before.

The Superstar competition represented a new high in the financial expectations of women athletes. For volleyball players everywhere, it represented a recognition of the athletic nature of an old sport that had been considered purely recreational. For Mary Jo Peppler, it represented the culmination of twelve long years of devotion to her favorite game.

*Normally a professional volleyball player, Mary Jo Peppler cycled her way to the first Women's Superstar crown at Rotonda, Florida, in 1975.* WIDE WORLD

# Index of Names